WHITE◆FOLKS' SOUL FOOD©

by: Richard Ford Thompson

Turtle Creek Press Dallas

Richard's Collection of White Folks' Soul Food.
Copyright ©1991 by Richard Ford Thompson.
All rights reserved.
Printed in the United States of America.
For information, write Turtle Creek Press, 500 East
Arapaho, Suite 107, Richardson, Texas 75081.
1 - 800 - 878-7508

Editor: Susan Turner
Cover/Book Design/Illustrations: Keith A. Gaston

Library of Congress Catalog Number: 91-66046
ISBN 1-880445-08-5

First Edition
10 9 8 7 6 5 4 3 2 1

Table of Contents

PREFACE	3
Chapter I	*7*
Magnificent Mashed Potatoes and Pork Roast	*8*
I Really Enjoy Good Soup	*11*
Easy Peanut Soup	*12*
Soup's On . . .	*12*
Adding Flavor	*14*
A Good Start	*15*
Chapter II	*17*
Sonora Chili	*17*
Chili for One	*17*
Beef Chili	*18*
Beans . . . Beans . . . Beans	*19*
Tomato Aspic	*19*
About Raisins	*20*
The World's Best Tuna Salad	*21*
Raisin - Corn Puddin'	*22*
Chapter III	*23*
Savory Pound Cake	*23*
Pineapple Upside-Down Cake	*24*
Richard's Famous German Chocolate	
Upside-Down Cake	*25*
Scones	*26*
Crumpets	*27*
Stuffed Sweet Cherry Peppers	*28*
Chili con Queso	*29*
Mother's Hors d'oeuvres	*29*
Party Dip	*30*
Rack Of Spam	*30*
Breakfast Muffins	*31*
Apple Spice Icebox Cake	*32*
Would Anybody Like Some Pie?	*32*
Banana Cream	*33*
Coconut Cream	*34*

Chapter IV — 35

- Poultry Plus — 35
- White Folks' Chicken — 36
- Hunter's Chicken or Chicken Cacciatore — 36
- Stuffing Or Dressing — 38
- Waldorf Salad — 40

Chapter V — 41

- Pigs -n- Blanket — 41
- Pig Sauce — 41
- The Original Breakfast Tacos — 42
- Easy Salsa — 42
- Garlic Sauce — 42
- The Absolute Best Bar-B-Q Beans — 43
- Cooked Cabbage — 44
- Really Good Brussels Sprouts — 44
- Catalina Carrot Coins — 45
- Tender Cooked Cauliflower — 45
- Richard's Cheese Sauce — 45
- Carrot Jell-o Salad — 46
- Oven Roastin' Corn — 46
- Alabama Corn Patties — 46
- Escalloped Corn — 47
- Pecan Pie etc., etc. — 48
- Old Fashioned Pecan — 48

Chapter VI — 49

- Kentucky Cheese Torte — 50
- Fudge Pie — 50
- Nutty-Cheese Toast — 51
- Mississippi Stir Fry Beef w/Greens — 51
- Jarlsberg Cheese Fondue — 53
- Cream Puff Ring — 54
- Oatmeal Pound Cake — 55
- A Great Dinner: — 57
- Orange Vinaigrette — 57
- My Orange Vinaigrette Salad — 57
- Pepper Beef Tenderloin — 57
- Smothered Baked Potatoes — 58

Chapter VII — 59

Is it Snack Time?	*59*
Shortbread Cookies	*59*
Old Fashioned Sand Tarts	*60*
Potato Pancakes	*61*
Penuche	*61*
Bread Pudding	*62*
Chicken Fried Steak	*63*
Richard's Chili	*64*
After School Muffins	*65*
Easy Tuna Casserole	*67*
Popcorn Puddin'	*68*
Breadstick Snacks	*69*
Gingerbread Cookies	*69*

Chapter VIII — *71*

Cole-n-Sak	*74*
Escalloped Pork Chops	*75*
Rice Krispic Treats	*75*
South Texas Pork Stew	*76*
Dallas Jambalaya	*77*
Italian Sausage Sauce	*78*
Easy Salmon Patties	*78*
Spicy Caper Mayonnaise	*79*
Nuked Zucchini	*80*

Chapter IX — *81*

Dorothy's Hummingbird Cake	*81*
Cream Cheese Frosting	82
Coco - Loco Pound Cake	82
Pot D'Creme — Egg Custard — Flan' Etc.	83
Chicken Pie Especial	*85*
Cheesie Chicken Casserole	86
Sweet Potato Pie	86
Whipped Cream	87
Pumpkin Pie	87
Great Northern Beans	87
Spiced Sauerkraut w/ Canadian Bacon	88

Chapter X — *89*

24 Hour Icebox Salad	*90*
Richard's Special Dressing	*90*
Cranberry Relish	*91*
Fresh Basil, Vinegar & Oil Dressing	*92*

Mouth Watering Pot Roast	*92*
Delicious Artichokes	*93*
Sweet Corn Relish	*94*
Green Bean Bundles	*95*
Padre Island Shrimp Roast	*96*
Summer Avocado Salad	*96*
Marinated Shrimp	*97*
Happy Birthday Puppa	*98*
Potpourri Jambalaya	*99*
Louisiana Cheese Crisps	*100*
Curry Cheese Spread	*101*
French Silk Pie	*101*
Baked Parmesan Cheese Noodles	*102*
Roma Meat Roll	*103*
Summer Stuffed Tomatoes	*104*

Chapter XI — *105*

Sacher Torte	*105*
Bess's Rye Rolls	*107*
Chicken in Plantation Sauce	*108*
Spinach in Mushroom Sauce	*109*
My Mama's Hot Quiche	*110*
Fresh Zucchini Salad	*110*
Russian Dressing	*111*
Mississippi Cheese Grits	*111*
Hershey Bar Pie	*112*
Graham Cracker Crust	*113*
Helpful Hints	*113*

Chapter XII — *115*

Almond Crescents	*115*
Strawberry Pie	*116*
Green Bean Casserole I	*116*
Green Bean Casserole II	*117*
Green Bean Casserole III	*117*
Old Time Chocolate Cake	*118*
Chocolate Icing	*119*
Cheddar Dip	*119*
Peanut Brittle	*120*
Reception Salad	*121*
Caviar Spread	*122*
Strawberry Ice Box Pie	*123*
Chocolate Ice Box Pie	*123*

Texas Tortilla Casserole	*124*
Coconut Raisin Oatmeal Cookies	*125*
Butterscotch Bars	*126*

Chapter XIII *127*

Key Lime Pie	*127*
German Chocolate Pie	*128*
Eagle Brand Brownies	*128*
Smoked Turkey Ball	*129*
Asparagus Salad	*129*
Tennessee Corn Casserole	*130*
Oatmeal Banana Nut Bread	*131*
Sweet Potato Casserole	*131*
Noel's Swiss Cheese Ball	*132*
Turnip Greens with Cornmeal Dumplings	*132*
Cashew Nut Butter	*134*
Virgina Honey Nut Butter	*134*
Richard's Pasta Salad	*135*
Pasta Salad Dressing	*135*
Cheese Rice Casserole	*136*
True Lasagna	*137*
Cranapple Muffins	*139*
Ham & Cheese Rollups	*140*

Chapter XIV *141*

Melba's Garlic Sweet Pickles	*141*
Richard's Garlic Dill Pickles	*142*
Corn Relish	*143*
Jalapeno Cornbread	*144*
Krazy Apple Krisp	*145*
Spanish Green Beans	*146*
Cream Cheese Pie	*147*
East Texas Brownies	*148*
Alabama Mushroom Chicken	*148*
Chocolate Nut Butter	*149*
Chili Rice	*150*
Georgia Sweet Potato Biscuits	*150*

Chapter XV *151*

Broccoli Rice Casserole	*151*
Texas Trash	*152*
Crustless Quiche	*153*
Cheese Soup	*154*

Remoulade Sauce	*155*
Chopped Liver	*155*
Dumplings	*156*
A Recipe For Life	*156*

Chapter XVI — *157*

Baked Ham Hash	*157*
Baking Powder Biscuits	*158*
Buttermilk Biscuits	*158*
Bean and Sausage Stew	*159*
Fried Green Tomatoes	*160*

Chapter XVII — *161*

Texas Tamales	*161*
Tamale Pie	*163*
Pico de Gallo	*164*

Chapter XVIII — *165*

Parmesan - Cream Cheese Spread	*165*
Italian Herbs	*166*
Black Bean Soup	*166*
Curry Chicken Salad with Melon	*167*
Things You Need	*168*
Grrrreat Flake Bars	*169*
Green Potato Soup	*169*
Hershey Dream	*170*
Pizza Pie	*171*
New Potato Salad	*172*
Crabmeat Cocktail	*173*
Steak Sauce	*174*

Chapter X1X — *175*

Broccoli Cornbread	*175*
Authentic Caesar Salad	*176*
Home Made Garlic Croutons	*176*
Alabama Corn Casserole	*177*
"Baked" Eggs With Hash	*178*
Brandied Mixed Fruit Spread	*178*
Louisiana Boiled Shrimp	*179*
New Orleans Style Shrimp Sauce	*179*
Neiman Marcus Spiced Tea	*180*

Chapter XX — *181*

Pico de Terry	*182*

Swiss Steak	*183*
Jarlsberg Tuna Melt	*184*
Cattleman's Meatloaf	*184*
Quick Brown Gravy	*185*
Buttered Yellow Squash	*185*
Chipped Beef	*186*
A Little Knowledge Helps	*187*
Richard's Unconventional Breakfast	*187*
Dessert Rice	*188*
Hot Buttered Pears	*188*

Chapter XXI — *189*

Morning Spiced Hot Cider	*189*
Diamond T Spiced Apple Juice	*189*
French Toast	*190*
Lemon - Cream Cheese Pound Cake	*191*
Pineapple Right Side Up Cake	*192*
"Coke" Cake	*193*
Spinach In Sour Cream	*194*
Salmon Croquettes	*194*
True Beef Stroganoff	*195*
Southern Baked Pork Cutlets	*196*

Chapter XXII — *197*

Neiman Marcus Poppy Seed Dressing	*197*
Eagle Brand Fudge	*198*
Easy Potatoes Au Gratin	*198*
Traditional Tuna Salad	*199*
Kentucky Style Potato Salad	*199*
Lillian's Salad	*200*
Muskogee Baked Chicken Legs	*201*
Old Fashion Mushroom Soup	*201*
Buttered Baguette Toast Rounds	*202*
Easy Broccoli Cheese Soup	*203*
Cream Gravy — Sausage Gravy — Etc.	*203*
White Sauce	*204*
Mother's Bread Puddin'	*205*
Marinated Pork Chops	*205*
A Different Green Bean Casserole	*206*

Chapter XXIII — **207**

Soul Food	*207*

INDEX — **208**

The intention of every other piece of prose may be discussed or even mistrusted; but the purpose of a cookery book is one and unmistakable. Its object can conceivably be no other than to increase the happiness of mankind.
— Joseph Conrad

PREFACE

I can't give you blue skies, majestic mountainsides, an ocean tide, or many of the wonders of the world. I can, however, share something of myself in the way of wonderfully delicious recipes that nourish the soul.

In each and every dish in this incredible collection, there is a part of me, my family, my friends and the earth itself. Soul food cooking is taking the resources available to us and refining them into delectable masterpieces through a process of love, harmony, and enjoyment.

Now, some people may define soul food as simply down-home or southern cooking —chicken fried steaks, gravy and biscuits, chittlins, etc. But this is not necessarily soul food. Soul food is the direct result of the way the food is cooked —no matter what it is. It is the attitude you yourself have when you cook the food and the enthusiasm you share with others involved in the process.

If cooking is viewed as nothing more than a monotonous daily task that is begrudgingly performed, both the food and partakers will reflect it. That is why two cooks can follow a recipe identically, and one will produce true soul food, and the other food that is barely edible. The difference lies in attitude. To the first cook, the preparation was a labor of love and enjoyment. To the second, it was a task and duty.

Soul Food is the best tasting, most appetizing and delicious food in the whole world. But you can't cook soul food if you really don't like to eat. Eating is not just stuffing down food; eating is a social event —a time to stop working and enjoy family and friends.

In today's high tech, fast-paced world, many people are forced to work harder and harder to make ends meet. For most of us, mealtime is probably our only breather, a time we can stop long enough to enjoy our existence and one another.

Let us break bread together.

One of the great things about soul food is that it neither calls for a countless number of ingredients nor great expense. Soul food cooking calls only for a good attitude and your own creative expression. It is cooking to make others happy by using whatever you have to the very best.

The best soul food is produced when you cook with someone —someone you can talk to and enjoy being with. This could be your child, husband or wife, a niece or nephew, a neighbor's child, or good friend.

As a child, I developed my love of cooking as a result of helping great cooks like Helen Corbitt, Odell Stewart, my great aunt Locky Mae Ford, "my Oma" Mrs. Fritz Steeler, Lillian Real, Roberta Smith, and Melba Luglan in their kitchens. As I chopped onions, celery, radishes, or whatever, I observed they did not cook for just the sake of cooking. They loved to cook, they delighted in pleasing others, and their enthusiasm was contagious.

From as early as I can remember, to me cooking was never a chore, but always fun, entertaining, and a loving experience.

Thus, the first and primary ingredient for soul food is attitude —being happy in what you're doing. If this is not the case, the soul is not right, and your meal will reflect it.

So if you're feeling angry, hostile, or bitter, don't cook. Go to Burger King or Jack in the Box. No one should ever attempt to cook anything unless he truly wants it to taste good and wants to share it with others.

With the right attitude, anyone can cook soul food. In fact, the only magic in being a good cook is the magic of being hungry. Because soul food cooking is actually your own expression, all you have to do is use your sense of taste. You know what you're hungry for. Simply put things together until they taste good. All you have to do is think, and as my friend Bill Proctor says:

Think if you can think.

In this book, you'll find many sumptuous recipes — some totally original, some modified from those passed down through the generations, and some created by family and friends.

This is a copyrighted collection, although I don't know why. Soul food is food that is meant to be shared.

So as the author, I hope that you will take the recipes and use them as I have written them and then change them to satisfy your taste, because I *want these recipes to become your recipes.*

I write this with the wish that my book will bring happiness to you, your family, and your friends.

Enjoy!

Richard F Thompson

Richard Ford Thompson

I

Soul Food cooking is not only fun; it's also a learning experience.

Much of the learning will involve the use of seasonings — a pragmatic trial and error approach. The easiest way to reduce errors is to think small, and I do mean small. All seasonings provide flavor —each with pleasure, but only when used in small pinches. Do not be afraid to add seasoning, but I can't be emphatic enough when I say, "keep it in very small amounts." Even those seasonings you like become overpowering if you use too much.

Soul Food cooking is creative cooking, an expression of youself. All the recipes here and in any other good cookbook are open to additions of seasonings to add a special touch, personalizing the dish for you and your family and friends.

In no way should cooking ever be considered a chemical formula that must be followed to a "T." Cooking that nourishes the soul is as individual as the preparer or the partakers. *Remember, if it tastes good, it is good.*

Taste is a faculty of the soul that discerns something good with pleasure.

Let's begin with mashed potatoes . . .

Magnificent Mashed Potatoes and Pork Roast
(Serves 6 to 8)

2 to 2 ½ pounds potatoes (either red or white)
1 stick butter
1½ cup milk
salt
pepper
¼ teaspoon grated ginger root
pork roast
water
garlic salt
½ cup flour
A-1 Sauce (optional)

Wash and peel potatoes (completely, or partially if you want peeling in the tators). Cut the tators in small (1") pieces and boil in salt water until tender (about 10 minutes). Drain and mash with butter, milk, salt, pepper, and (to add a special flavor) ¼ teaspoon grated ginger root.

Serve this with pan gravy from a pork roast.

To cook a pork roast, you'll need a covered roasting pan. Pour about 1 to 1 ½ cups of water into the pan and place the roast fat side up in the water. Cover the fat with a liberal amount of garlic salt and cook in a fast preheated oven — 400° to 450° — until the fat turns light brown. During the first 1 to 1½ hours, check the roast about every 30 minutes to make sure the water hasn't cooked away.

Add approximately a cup of water at a time to the pan (not over the roast). After the first hour-and-a-half, check the roast more frequently.

The size of the roast doesn't make any difference in the cooking procedure. It is the method I give you that's important.

Pan gravy is made by removing the roast from the pan and adding ½ cup flour to the drippings. Stir to mix well. Then place the roasting pan on a burner and heat to bubbling while stirring constantly. Add salt and fresh ground pepper to taste. If you like, add a teaspoon of A-1 Sauce to your gravy to enhance the flavor. Use milk to thin as necessary.

It is not the intent of this book to offer recipes with strict directions on how to prepare an item. Instead this book is about how to put things together to create your own style of soul food cooking. Although I enthusiastically share my thoughts on what goes well together, these are examples only and not cast in concrete. It's the way I do it. You do it your way.

In this book, you'll find suggestions on things ranging from cooking for a large gathering to stretching your food budget, while saving storage space in the process.

When cooking gravy, for example, stop after you mix the flour and drippings into a smooth paste. Do not add water or milk to thin out into gravy. Instead, refrigerate the paste itself in a smaller storage bowl, and have gravy all week long. Merely heat two-to-three tablespoons of the paste per serving and thin with water or milk for instant gravy.

> *This book is not your typical cookbook. It is written for you to cook your way. You will not find foods classified or grouped together in sections, but I encourage you to keep a supply of index cards handy and put recipes in a personal file. If fixing something you are unfamiliar with, you may wish to follow the directions the first time and later change to suit your taste. On your recipe card,* **write it your way.**
>
> *There is nothing within this book that I claim sole credit for. I have merely watched and learned since I was very young.*

Good cooking does not have to be hard and time consuming. I will give you a number of short cuts which I have found to make cooking easier. If you don't make a lot of desserts, for example, mixes may be more practical for you than scratch ingredients which can get old, stale, or lose their strength.

I Really Enjoy Good Soup.

Here are some ways you can turn canned soup into really good soup by using leftovers.

First of all, when purchasing canned soup, buy Campbell or Progresso or a good name brand. You will know the difference if you try less expensive store brands, and really won't save if the taste is not there. On some items, you can buy store brands and save; but soup is not one of them.

In many instances, there may be a small amount of a veggie leftover; and even if it has dried out a little in the refrigerator, you can add it to a can of soup, and it will work well.

Examples are:

(a) Macaroni & cheese — add to Campbell Tomato made with milk

(b) Macaroni & cheese — add to Progresso Lentil, or Campbell's or Progresso's Vegetable soup.

(c) Black-eyed peas, cream peas or purple hulls —add to Progresso Tomato or Vegetable Soup.

(d) Squash, carrots, beans, or even cabbage — add to lentil or vegetable soup

(e) Broccoli — add to cream of chicken or corn chowder

When using canned soups, I recommend adding a teaspoon of butter to enhance the flavor. Start out by using a little less water or milk to make a heartier soup (you can always thin it if needed). . . . And I always make *cream* soups with *milk* not water.

Easy Peanut Soup

In the deep South peanut soup is popular, and was made popular world wide by the late Helen Corbitt, director of Neiman Marcus Restaurants. I found that I could duplicate Helen's recipe by adding 2 or 3 tablespoons of crunchy peanut butter to a can of cream of chicken soup. I like Progresso Cream of Chicken with Mushrooms best for this, but for variation, use corn chowder.

When you are adding veggies to canned soup, you may prefer to use bullion instead of water...but when mixing bullion cubes, always eliminate other salt as the cubes are salty. I use a lot of bullion cubes in both soups and gravy, but it does replace a lot of the salt.

Soup's On . . .

Now, for large pots of soup, you can start with the many types of beans— navy, butter, pinto, red — and peas —black- eyed, purple hull, field, etc.— and ham. Here is where a name brand doesn't matter. You can buy the least expensive ham in the store, have the butcher grind it for you; and whether you are cooking the beans as a veggie or making soup, the boiling ham will flavor and be tender.

To start, put the ham in the pot at low temperature to render some of the fat. ***Do not cook on high***. Now, as the fat begins to render, put in a chopped onion or two and a cup or two of chopped celery and let simmer for a few minutes. Then add the beans or peas and water, a little salt and pepper. Cook at low boil for at least 1 ½ hours until the beans are just tender. Now add water, if needed, and a package of frozen mixed veggies (here again you can use the store brand or least expensive package) and cook about an hour longer. ***Watch your water level and cook slowly enough to prevent sticking on bottom.***

When veggies are tender, add Ramen Noodles (chicken or beef). Before opening the noodles, however, crush package to break noodles into small pieces, and you will have a hearty soup.

Note: If you want a tomato taste, you can use a can of tomato or V-8 juice *after the beans are cooked* instead of adding water.

Also check the refrigerator when making a large pot of soup and add any veggies that may be just sitting there.

Remember that cabbage and brussels sprouts are very strong tasting veggies, and if you add these, you will very certainly taste them in the soup.

I do not recommend measured or specified ingredients in making soup in that soup is truly the use of what is there, and you should use what you and yours like.

My soup has always been eaten heartily by adults, teens, and children. I have more luck at having everyone like the soup than almost anything else that is fixed for a large group (except for chocolate chip cookies). Soup also freezes well for up to six months.

If beans are initially cooked as a veggie, use left over cooked beans in soup. It is a good idea to cook the mixed veggies slowly, as the beans will tend to thicken the soup and scorch if cooked too fast.

Another way to cook beans is with bacon or salt pork. Cut the pork into small pieces; wash and cook in the pot until it renders its fat or the bacon is crisp. Then add chopped onion and celery and perhaps a carrot or two; cook for a few minutes before adding the beans, water, salt, and pepper, and slow boil for several hours (watching the water level) until beans are tender.

Adding Flavor

Here I want to talk of cooking with salt. I use Vege-Sal, which is an all natural salt with a subtle taste.

I also use Mrs. Dash and Lawry's salt, but they have stronger flavors. I am also apt to use basil, rosemary, thyme, cilantro, and other herbs and seasonings in my beans, soups and other dishes. As the mood hits you, experiment. Just remember a little bit can go a long way. Be exceptionally careful with curry and oregano in that they are very strong. A pinch means a small pinch.

To accompany soup, plain crackers are always good, but if you prefer cornbread, I suggest using Jiffy Cornbread Mix. Mixed as directed, it is a no fail mix and . . . soooo easy and good. . . To make it spicier, you could add a small can of whole or cream corn, a chopped jalapeno or two, and perhaps ¾ cup of cheddar cheese to the cornbread mix.

Unless you are using an old-fashioned cast iron cornbread pan (which you heat in a 450° oven, grease with bacon drippings and put the batter in the smoking hot pan).....then use BAKERS JOY SPRAY (not Pam or other sprays), as Bakers Joy contains flour and will positively prevent sticking of baking breads, cakes, muffins, etc.

A Good Start

Another way to start a large pot of soup is with a beef soup bone, which has been cut (sawed) by the butcher so the marrow of the bone is exposed. Place soup bone and 1 pound of lentils in a large pot of water (at least a 6 quart and preferably a 10 quart) and bring to a rolling boil. Then turn down heat for a gentle boil and skim the foamy stuff off the top.

Cook for at least two hours. Remove bone, and skim again if necessary; and add a large can of V-8 juice, a large can of tomatoes (cut up), and a package of frozen mixed veggies. Cook about an hour, and add 1 ½ pounds potatoes, cut in small pieces, and cook another hour.

.... Now this has said nothing of seasonings ... When you add the juice and veggies, you can add Vege-Sal, cracked pepper, a pinch of rosemary, or thyme or basil, or a bayleaf or two as you like, but use seasonings sparingly. Oregano is too strong for soup, unless you want minestrone, and then use only a very small amount. Again, with a large pot of soup, adjust to what you have and what your family likes. Add a hand full of small or large navy beans when starting the lentils or a hand full of butter beans or kidney beans, (but since I don't like kidneys I won't mention them often).

When you add the potatoes, you can add spaghetti or macaroni or noodles of any kind, or you can add okra, (which I love) but know your crowd before you put okra in the soup. (Beets & turnips do not do well in soup).

To those of you who have not done much cooking:

You may think that I stress small amounts of seasoning too much, but let me say that the best cooking is food that is well seasoned, while the worst cooking is food that is over seasoned.

When grilling hamburger patties (or frying them), for example, sprinkle a little oregano on the patties. But *if you have leftovers to freeze, do not sprinkle with oregano,* for it seems to get stronger in the freezer.

II

Chili is a large red pepper which can be cooked whole or ground in to powder. Then there's:

> *Chili Con Carne — chili with meat*
> *Chili con Queso — chili with cheese*
> *Chili - - usually refers to Chili Con Carne,*
>   *but when traveling, ask.*

Sonora Chili

Sonora chili begins with *several leg quarters of chicken, a large whole chili for each, an onion chopped for each, a carrot sliced for each, a garlic pod for the pot, and salt.* Cook at a rolling boil until chicken is tender and falls off the bones. Then remove bones and the skin from the pot and add *a diced potato for each leg quarter and a can of tomatoes (cut up)* and cook till the tators are done — this will be a thin soup.

Chili for One

If you want chili for one, a *can of Wolf brand (WITHOUT BEANS)* is always good. In fact, I don't recommend any canned chili with beans . . .

Beef Chili

If you want beef chili, get the *Two Alarm mix* and use 1 & ½ times the recommended meat, using the least expensive *ground beef* you can buy. Do not drain grease, but cook chili completely and place pan in the refrigerator. After the grease is hard, skim off the top.

> Note: If chili is thick, add water to bring the grease to the top; the water can be cooked down if chili is too thin when you take the grease off.

Wick Fowler has done a commendable job in packaging chili seasonings for good chili.

For good pinto beans to go with chili, I suggest cooking pintos with only water and salt, as this will give you the true bean flavor, which complements the other flavors already in your chili. Cook the beans separately, but you can serve mixed, or serve a mixture of chili and beans over a bed of brown rice with sliced onion on the side.

When slicing onion for the table, do it 15 minutes before serving. Set the slices in a bowl, and cover with ice. This always seems to give onions a fresh crisp taste.

As for the rice, I would like to relate that I prefer brown rice, for its nutty taste, with chili and red beans. White rice, to me, has a softer taste which I prefer with gravy and most certainly in rice pudding.

Beans . . . Beans . . . Beans

Red Beans are not Kidney Beans. They are RED BEANS which may be hard to find. (You can substitute pinto if you can't find red).

Cook your red beans with water, garlic, and salt until tender.

In a skillet, cook ground beef, seasoned with garlic salt and crushed red pepper, until the meat is well done and crumbles easily; skim off most of the grease and add to the beans; cook at low boil for 10 or 15 minutes and serve over brown rice with corn bread.

These beans are great in the morning, heated, with a fried egg over the top. I like a toasted English muffin with them.

With soup or beans, a salad is always great. Now, I'm not going to tell anyone how to make a green salad or what dressing to use - - just do it.

But if you don't want a green salad, how 'bout *tomato aspic?*

Tomato Aspic

a 46 ounce can V-8 Juice
one envelope Knox Gelatin
a small box lemon Jell-o
a tablespoon Lea & Perrin

In a two cup measuring cup, pour out about one cup of V-8, and mix will with Knox Gelatin and lemon Jell-o. Pour into pan with the rest of the V-8; and bring to a low boil, stirring all the time. Remove from heat; add a tablespoon of Lea & Perrin, and you have aspic. Pour in molds or a pyrex dish to put in the refrigerator.

This is basic. Now read for additions and make your choice.

Aspic can have many additions. I like Cara Mia marinated artichoke hearts or hearts of palm, tiny green peas, chopped celery, etc. Ordinarily I add only one item to my aspic and serve it with one cup of mayonnaise, to which I add the juice of a lemon and about ¼ teaspoon Lawry's salt.

About Raisins

Plumped Raisins

If you don't like raisins because they are tough and gummy when they are dry, try this. Take about 1 or 1 ½ cup of raisins and put them in a sauce pan with 2 jiggers of sweet liquor — i.e sherry, brandy, Meyers rum, any other dark rum, Frangelico, Amaretto, or maybe a jigger each of two kinds — 2 or 3 tablespoons of sugar, and enough water to just barely cover the raisins.

Put on very high heat and bring to a fierce boil for only a few seconds. Remove from heat, cover with tight lid, and let the pan cool. You will have raisins that are plump and flavorful.

When raisins are cool, drain juice and add to 1 pound of shredded carrots. Then add mayonnaise for a delicious carrot & raisin salad.

You can also add these raisins to oatmeal for breakfast or anything else that calls for raisins.

THE WORLD'S BEST TUNA SALAD

1 can water packed tuna
(Preferably - white albacore)
¾ cup chopped pecans
½ cup chopped celery
½ can sliced water chestnuts, cut into small pieces
¾ cup plumped raisins
about 4 or 5 tablespoons mayonnaise.

Mix all the ingredients together and refrigerate for about an hour before serving. Adjust mayonnaise to consistency desired.

Use the other half can of water chestnuts to add to a can of whole green beans as a hot veggie.

Words of Wisdom

>*God gave us two ends - - one to think with and one to sit on...Your success in life depends upon which you use the most.*
>   — With thanks to my mother.

Raisin - Corn Puddin'

about ¾ cup of plumped raisins
4 cups fresh corn and juice, scraped from the cob
1 cup sugar
½ stick of butter
1 & ½ cups milk
¼ teaspoon each, nutmeg & cinnamon.

Heat butter, milk, and sugar together. Then add remaining ingredients and blend well. Pour into a greased glass baking pan and bake at 350° for 30 - to - 40 minutes. Pudding will be slightly firm.

As a vegetable . . .

Omit sugar, raisins, nutmeg, and cinnamon.

Add 1 medium chopped onion

Melt butter in sauce pan, and cook a medium chopped onion until it is clear (Cook slowly, so as not to scorch the butter or onion). Add corn & juice, salt, and cracked pepper. Blend and bake as above.

Depending on the sweetness of your corn, you might add a tablespoon of sugar to this vegetable.

III

How 'bout a good pound cake?

Savory Pound Cake

1 pound real butter
4 cups cake flour
½ teaspoon cream of tartar
½ teaspoon salt
3 cups sugar
9 or 10 eggs depending on size
1 teaspoon vanilla
Baker's Joy Spray

Preheat your oven to 300° degrees. Put one pound of butter, and I do mean butter (not margarine) in a large bowl and let it come to room temperature.

While butter is softening, sift together 4 cups of good cake flour, ½ teaspoon cream of tartar, and ½ teaspoon salt. Sift again and set aside.

To the softened butter, add 3 cups sugar and mix well. Then add the eggs — two at time, mixing as you go. After you have mixed in all the eggs, add 1 teaspoon vanilla and mix again.

Now the sifted flour may be added, a little at a time, mixing well before adding more. Batter should be smooth — no lumps.

Cook your pound cake in either a loaf pan or a tube pan *(I prefer tube pan)*. Pan should be well coated by Baker's Joy or well greased & floured.

If using a loaf pan, use either two pans or a long pan. If you use a large bread loaf pan, the cake will not get done in the center. Bake the cake for 1½ hours at 300°. Do not cook too fast, for this cake cooks slowly in the middle.

Some like a hint of lemon extract added to the butter mixture (3 or 4 drops), but try this cake without the lemon first.

This is a great cake, but it is work . . . So what? It's worth it.

For a really easy treat, try ...

Pineapple Upside-Down Cake

½ stick margarine
1 small can pineapple
1 cup light brown sugar
one yellow cake mix prepared
according to directions on box

Put ½ stick softened margarine in a square pyrex pan, and smear it over the bottom and sides. Next sprinkle a cup of light brown sugar on bottom and a small can crushed pineapple (the one about the size of a tuna can).

Add a good yellow cake mix, prepared according to directions, and bake as directed on the box. It is important, however, that you cool only six or seven minutes and turn upside-down onto the serving plate.

You may need to scrape some of the topping out of the pan and spread on cake while warm. Let cake cool and serve with Cool-Whip.

If there is any left, which is highly unlikely, watch it disappear at breakfast with orange juice and crisp bacon.

Hint: *For better results in baking, set eggs out and let them come to room temperature before using them.*

Now for an indescribably delicious cake — possibly the best you've ever eaten or ever will eat — try...

Richard's Famous German Chocolate Upside-Down Cake

½ stick margarine
1 ½ cups chopped pecans
1 cup of coconut
German chocolate cake mix
¼ pound margarine
1 box of powdered sugar
1 - 8 ounce package of cream cheese

Smear 1/2 stick of softened margarine over bottom and sides of an 8 x 8 pyrex. Spread 1 & ½ cups chopped pecans and a cup of coconut on bottom. Prepare a German Chocolate cake mix, according to instructions on the box, and pour on top.

Now here's the good part:

Add a mixture of ¼ pound margarine, powdered sugar, and cream cheese; spoon evenly on top of the cake batter, and bake at 350° for about an hour. Test center with toothpick before removing. Cooking time may be slightly longer, depending on the oven.

Cool about 6 or 7 minutes, and turn upside-down onto serving plate. Scrape any topping left in pan, and spread it onto cake as necessary. Cool completely and frost with white icing or serve as is.

People have told me that this cake "is to die for".

Scones

2 cups self rising flour
½ teaspoon baking soda
¾ cup buttermilk
1 egg yolk
sugar
Optional: ¾ cup plumped raisins

Scones are easy with this method. You sift two cups self-rising flour into large mixing bowl. Stir ½ teaspoon baking soda into ¾ cup buttermilk until it foams. Then pour into a well in the center of the flour and stir with a fork just enough to make a dough.

Scoop dough into a ball, and place on a lightly floured board. Pat into a circle, lightly kneading. Cut the circle into 10 wedges, and bake on a greased baking sheet 10 to 12 minutes at 350°.

To give the scones a golden shine, brush tops with an egg yolk, beaten with a tablespoon of water.

For a treat, add ¾ cup plumped raisins to the dough and then after brushing top with milk (not egg), sprinkle sugar on the top of the scones.

While we are obviously into tea time, let me say that crumpets are much more time consuming.

To make crumpets you need metal rings about the size of tuna cans. These may be hard to find since you can't cut both ends out of many of the cans being made today. You do, however, need to look for cans that you can make rings out of, as there will be several times you will need the rings (or buy the rings at a restaurant supply.)

Crumpets

1 package dry yeast
½ teaspoon sugar
2 ½ cups flour
a pinch of salt
Warm tap water (not hot)

In a small bowl, mix sugar and yeast with three tablespoons lukewarm water (this means water that is warm to the touch, not so hot you can't touch it). Place the bowl in the oven, **which is off.**

Sift flour and salt into a large bowl, and make a well in the center of the flour. Now add the yeast mixture and then ⅔ cup warm tap water. Beat hard for at least three minutes.

Cover the bowl with a cloth, and let stand in a warm place for about 45 minutes.

Beat down the dough, and add water to bring to the consistency of pancake batter. To cook, oil the rings and the skillet or griddle, and pour batter in rings. Remove rings when the tops start to bubble, and turn with a spatula as you would a thick pancake.

Drain your crumpets on paper towels, and they will keep about a week in the refrigerator. I like to reheat them in a cast iron skillet on low heat and serve with unsalted butter and a *GOOD* strawberry jam. (Please do spend the money for a good jam. You will be glad you did.)

Now here is one of my all-time favorite party treats

Stuffed Sweet Cherry Peppers

Bottle of cherry peppers (30 to 40 peppers)
1 pound hot Owens sausage
1 egg
30 crushed saltines

Pare the stem and remove the seeds from cherry peppers. Mix together sausage, egg, and crushed saltines. Stuff the meat mixture into the peppers, and bake 15 minutes in a 375 oven. Remove from oven; drain juice right away, and let the peppers sit for 5 minutes before serving.

For variation, use ground beef or chicken or turkey, seasoning it with onion, sage, thyme, oregano, Tabasco, etc.

For example, try ground chicken seasoned with only salt and a little black pepper.

Chili con Queso

When you serve Chili con Queso, first decide what chips you will be using. If you plan to serve Fritos (and I love Fritos) then you need to start with American cheese from the deli, and be sure that there isn't too much salt in the cheese. If you use tortilla chips, then you can use Velveeta cheese, which is salty.

Melt 1 pound cheese with a 16 ounce bottle of Tom Thumb Brand Picante Sauce (your choice of mild, medium, or hot) in either a double boiler or crock pot. A small crock pot not only works well, but you can serve your guests directly from it. If necessary, add a little water to keep the dip properly thin.

Mother's Hors d'oeuvres

One of my mother's favorites is to cook a pound of sausage till it crumbles, and drain it well. Spread slices of party rye bread on a cookie sheet. Put a spoon of sausage on each and cover with a slice of Swiss cheese (get the Swiss from the deli and have it sliced sandwich thin; the sliced Swiss in the dairy case is too thick). Broil until the cheese melts, which is not very long, and serve warm.

Note: If you rye is too large, cut it in half; use thin sliced rye.

Party Dip

As a dip for veggies, I like Marie's Ranch the best. It is usually found with the produce, but because there are so many prepared dressings for dips, just go to the store and pick your fancy.

You might even surprise your guests by serving veggies with mayonnaise, sprinkled with a little Paprika.

Neiman Marcus In-Circle asked for recipes and here are a couple which I submitted:

Rack Of Spam

The first secret to a good rack of spam is to pick a well marbled spam - if you need help ask your grocer (but only if he is over 50).

Preheat the oven to 400° on broil.

Score the spam lengthwise with a sharp knife, making your cuts about ½ into the spam. You will want three cuts. Next force strips of cheese into the cuts so that the top of the spam is fanned out.

Make a sauce of *¼ cup catsup, 1 teaspoon yellow mustard, 1 teaspoon Worcestershire, and a few drops Tabasco.* Turn oven up to 450 to get the broiler hot. Spoon the sauce over the top of the spam and place in the oven for 8 - 10 minutes to brown the top and melt the cheese.

Slice crosswise and serve with pork 'n beans.

While we are on spam . . . for breakfast meat, slice spam lengthwise about ¼ inch thick; get your skillet hot and put a little bacon grease in it. When it starts to smoke, it is ready. Fry the spam just to sear the outside and turn once. It should be crisp on the outside and tender on the inside.

To barbecue spam, punch holes in it. Spread a teaspoon of liquid smoke on it and place in a 300° oven for 20 to 25 minutes until it is good and hot.

Drain the excess spam juice and cover the spam with ½ cup barbecue sauce and return to the oven for 10 minutes. Slice thin and serve with the barbecue sauce.

It goes well with corn on the cob and white beans.

The other really good recipe I submitted to *Neimans* is so easy, yet it is so good you won't believe it:

Breakfast Muffins

In a large bowl mix together - according to the package directions on each package:

1 box Jiffy Cornbread Mix
1 Duncan Hines Yellow Cake Mix.

This makes about 24 muffins, but . . . ***they won't last long.***

This is an easy cake. . . .

Apple Spice Icebox Cake

2 apples
spice cake mix
¼ cup lemon juice
½ pint sour cream
1 can Eagle Brand Milk
cinnamon

Spray a 9x13 pyrex pan with with Bakers Joy. Peel, core, and finely chop two apples. Mix with a spice cake mix; bake and leave in pan.

Top with a mixture of ¼ cup bottled lemon juice, ½ pint sour cream and a can of Eagle Brand. Return to oven for 10 minutes. Then remove and sprinkle cinnamon over the top and let cake cool. Put in refrigerator until serving time because this cake is best cold.

Would Anybody Like Some Pie?

When I told people I was writing a cookbook, everyone seemed to have suggestions. Now I know I should not start this argument, but I can't help but suggest the very best pie crust you have ever had. Pies are always judged upon their crust, that is unless you make a really bad filling (which is hard to do if you cook at all). Thus, the test is your crust. That's why I encourage you to at least try my recipe.

The World's Best Pie Crust

You'll need a food processor with the chopping blade in it. Now put in the following:

1 ½ cup flour
¼ cup Crisco
¼ cup unsalted butter
¼ teaspoon salt
1 tablespoon sugar

Turn food processor on and off to mix until your mixture looks like coarse sand. Then add ICE water a little at a time (about ¼ cup is all you will need and maybe less) to form a dough ball.

> Hint: if you put Crisco and butter in refrigerator and get them really cold before you start, you won't need to refrigerate the dough ball before you roll it out.

Roll out dough to about 1/8 inch thickness on lightly floured board.

If you try this recipe and don't agree that this is the very best pie crust you have ever made, what can I say? *You did follow my directions, didn't you? ....*

To bake the shell, prick the bottom and bake at 425° for 15 to 18 minutes (10 minutes for a partially baked shell that will be used for quiche).

Here are two quick, easy pies:

Banana Cream

To make a banana cream pie, bake your crust and select two fairly ripe bananas. Slice the bananas and squeeze lemon juice over them. Allow them to drain while you make a box of Jell-o Vanilla Pudding (the cooked type).

Spread the bananas on the bottom of the crust, pour the pudding over them, and chill in refrigerator at least an hour. Top with whipped cream and serve.

Coconut Cream

You can make a coconut cream pie by adding ½ cup of coconut to a package of vanilla pudding as above. Cool and serve with whipped cream topping.

> Note: I recommend vanilla pudding in that I do not like artificial fruit flavoring in pudding.

The desire accomplished is sweet to the soul.

— Proverbs 13:19

IV

Good Food and Good Friends, when mixed together, make a lasting relationship...

While passion may change or fade away,
you will always get hungry
(to your dying day.)

So share your meals with a friend for lasting happiness. I truly say that you will stay happier if you keep your family and friends together with good meals.

In today's fast pace, let us not stop eating together. Even if you catch a fast meal at a fast food joint (which I certainly hope is not often), do it with someone you enjoy being with.

Poultry Plus

For any chicken dish, use what you like —dark, white, skin-on, or skin-off— but remember that the skin keeps in the moisture. If you remove the skin, you must baste more often, cook slower and longer, and watch so you don't brown the chicken; or it will be tough. I like to cook chicken with the skin on and remove it before serving. The dark quarters need to cook a little longer (due to larger bones).

White Folks' Chicken

Mix a tablespoon of yellow mustard, a tablespoon of cider vinegar, four tablespoons margarine, and ½ teaspoon salt. Rub the mixture onto 4 chicken quarters and place the chicken in a pyrex pan (9x13). Sprinkle about a cup of white bread crumbs over the chicken. Bake in a preheated 375° oven for about 40 minutes Scrape the crumbs off the skin into the juice and discard the skin. Spoon the crumbs and juice over the chicken and serve.

Hunter's Chicken
or
Chicken Cacciatore

6 whole boneless chicken breasts
or
a whole cut-up chicken
or
4 leg quarters (your choice)

5 - 6 large fresh mushrooms or 1 small can
½ tablespoon crushed thyme (use fresh if you can get it)
2 cups fresh tomatoes, chopped and skinned
¼ cup olive oil
one garlic pod
one large onion, chopped
½ cup dry white wine
1 small can tomato paste
½ teaspoon allspice
2 tablespoons grated lemon rind

The Italian word for *"Hunter"* is *"Cacciatore"*, hence the name of this great dish which goes well with spaghetti or egg noodles.

For this dish, I like fresh mushrooms. You can pick about 5 or 6 from the bulk mushrooms. The way to choose mushrooms is to look under the heads and see that they are closed (If none of the brown ribbing is showing, they are fresh). Also if using thyme leaves, crumble (*but not to powder*) enough for about ½ tablespoon.

First bring about 2 quarts of water to a boil, and briefly dip tomatoes in the hot water to loosen the skin. Remove skin, and chop enough fresh tomatoes to make 2 cups.

In a large skillet, put ¼ cup olive oil and a mashed garlic pod. Cook until brown. Then remove the garlic, and add chopped onion. When the onion starts to get clear, add dry white wine, tomato paste, chopped tomatoes, allspice, and crumbled thyme leaves (if using canned thyme, reduce to ½ teaspoon as it is so finely crushed). Add salt and fresh ground pepper to taste, and finely chopped mushrooms.

Rub a casserole dish with oil, and arrange chicken (preferably skinless chicken breasts) in it. Pour sauce over chicken; cover, and bake at 350° for about 1 hour and 15 minutes. Grate a lemon rind on top, and serve.

This can also be cooked in a large deep skillet on the top of the stove. Use a cut-up chicken, but cook slow, just to the bubbling point for about an hour or so. Watch sauce, and if it starts to get too thick, add water.

STUFFING OR DRESSING

In a skillet, melt ¼ pound margarine and cook a large chopped onion and ½ cup chopped celery until the onion is clear. Mix with:

> 2 cups bread crumbs
> 3 cups corn bread crumbs
> ½ teaspoon fresh ground pepper and salt to taste
> ½ teaspoon sage
> two cups chicken or turkey stock

Cook in 9x13 Pyrex dish at 350° for about 45 minutes.

The above is the basic recipe, and variations below can be added as you like. In fact, you can be very creative in your additions.

My favorite is:

> 1 pound hot sausage
> 1 cup chopped pecans
> 1 cup chopped fresh mushrooms

Other additions are:

> ½ cup "plumped" raisins
> 2 cups oysters
> 1 cup cooked corn (cream style or whole kernel)
> 1 ½ cups chopped apple
> 1 cup chopped walnuts
> ½ cup ground almonds

Or

Try this:

Cut the basic recipe in half and add 1 & ½ pound ground beef and 1 teaspoon Lawry salt. To serve, stuff either bell peppers, tomatoes or eggplant.

For hors d'oeuvres, stuff mushroom caps.

Now, if you are in a hurry, use two envelopes Stovetop cornbread stuffing mix. Add 1 pound hot sausage and 1 cup chopped pecans **Cut the water in half** and bake in 350° oven for 30 minutes.

Hint: When mixing sausage, mix with the bread crumbs until well mixed so there are no sausage lumps in your dressing.

Dressing goes very well with a pork roast and can be complemented with mint jelly.

If making dressing for duck, try the apple dressing with the grated rind of about ½ lemon.

or

raisin & apple with the grated rind of an orange.

Now don't just serve dressing at Thanksgiving and Christmas. Dressing is good all year round. *If this were not so, why would we eat it on special occasions?*

Waldorf Salad

First mix dressing:

>½ cup mayonnaise
>½ cup sour cream
>3 tablespoons sugar

Stir together, and set aside while preparing the rest of the salad.

>2 cups unpeeled diced red apples
>1 cup diced unpeeled yellow (or green) apples
>1 ½ cup thinly sliced celery
>1 ½ cup mini marshmallows
>1 cup pecan pieces (not broken too finely)
>½ cup maraschino cherry halves
>(If Christmas use both red & green)

Mix all together, and toss with dressing to coat well. Refrigerate for 30 minutes; then toss again. Before serving, refrigerate for at least an hour longer *(overnight is best)*.

V

Pigs -n- Blanket

Pigs-n-blanket are a favorite of both my children and their friends.

Preheat oven to 375°. You'll need a one pound package of Oscar Meyer Little Smokies and a can of refrigerator biscuits. Cut each biscuit into three parts and stretch with fingers until ⅓ biscuit will wrap around one of the sausages. Pop in the oven and watch so you don't burn the bottoms. Bake about 7 - 8 minutes until just light brown.

Pig Sauce

When you are serving Pig-n-Blanket as an hors d'oeuvre, a great sauce is to blend 2 tablespoons of dry mustard, 1 teaspoon flour, and ¼ cup light cream or half & half well. Set aside and heat ¾ cup light cream or half & half. Then stir in mustard mixture.

In a separate bowl, beat an egg yolk and add a couple of tablespoons of the mustard mixture to the yolk and mix well, before combining with the whole mixture.

Add 1 teaspoon sugar and cook, stirring constantly until thickened. Stir in ½ cup cider vinegar,(heated in a small sauce pan first), and salt to taste.

The Original Breakfast Tacos

Breakfast Tacos take more work, but you don't have to eat them only for breakfast.

Start by frying one pound of diced potatoes in oil until brown and crisp. Place on paper towel and set aside.

Next, in a large deep skillet, crumble and brown two pounds hot sausage and a large diced onion. Skim off grease, and add the potatoes and six beaten eggs. Stir to keep the mixture from sticking too much.

Now fill a flour tortilla with the mixture and a generous amount of grated cheese. Fold or roll up the tortilla and place on a cookie sheet. When ready to serve, pop in a 400° oven for no more than five minutes and serve with salsa.

Easy Salsa

A quick salsa is to pour a can of Rotel in the blender. Add a teaspoon of garlic salt and two whole pickled jalapenos and blend smooth.

Garlic Sauce

Here is a great garlic sauce, which is wonderful for veggies and is great on fish such as grilled tuna steak.

In a food processor with the metal blade, put 6 peeled garlic pods and ½ teaspoon salt; and process to a paste. Next add 3 egg yolks, and process to mix well. Now begin to add 1½ cups olive oil, a few drops at a time, until the sauce starts to thicken.

Then add the oil slowly in a thin stream; after all the oil is added, add one tablespoon strained lemon juice.

Refrigerate this if you don't use it right away.

and . . . Speaking of Veggies . . .

THE ABSOLUTE BEST BAR-B-Q BEANS

THESE ARE MY SWEET - HOT BAR-B-Q BEANS WHICH ARE WITHOUT QUESTION THE BEST YOU WILL EVER EAT.

Take one pound sliced bacon and cut crosswise in about one inch pieces. Put in a large, deep skillet and cook slowly until bacon just begins to get crisp. Add a large chopped onion (or two medium) and cook until the onion is clear. Add ½ pound dark brown sugar, a bottle catsup (the size you find in a cafe), 4 or 5 chopped pickled jalapenos, and 4 cans pork-n-beans.

Slowly simmer for about an hour, stirring to be sure it doesn't stick (if it sticks, turn down heat).

You can cut this in half, but don't try to cook only one can of beans, as you will eat one by yourself.

I like to eat these beans with cooked cabbage or brussels sprouts, both of which I like cooked to what most cookbooks would call over cooked.

Cooked Cabbage

To cook cabbage, I wash and cut a head into wedges and place in a pot with a couple of tablespoons bacon drippings, ½ teaspoon salt, ½ teaspoon sugar, and a little fresh ground pepper.

Start slowly, so it will begin making its own juice. If it isn't making enough, then add about a cup of water and cook with the lid on until the cabbage is very tender.

Really Good Brussels Sprouts

Start with about ½ pound *fresh* brussels sprouts if possible, but frozen will work. Put in pot with 2 tablespoons margarine, a pinch of salt, a pinch of sugar, fresh ground pepper, and about ½ cup water. Cover tightly and cook till the sprouts are tender, watching to see you don't cook away the water and burn the sprouts.

Now if you read other cookbooks, you will see these vegetables cooked in a pot of boiling water and only cooked a little so they remain firm and a little crisp, but I think my way is better.

Try it and see if someone who thinks they don't like cabbage or brussels sprouts won't say they like 'em this way . . . especially if you serve them with the sweet hot bar-b-q beans.

Catalina Carrot Coins

Carrot coins are made by skinning about a pound of carrots and slicing into thin coins. Put them in a large pickle jar (approx. 2 quarts) and fill with hot tap water. Heat a large bottle of Kraft Catalina French dressing in sauce pan until it begins to simmer.

Drain water from carrots; pour the catalina dressing over carrots, and let them sit on drain board until cool. Put lid on jar, and refrigerate over night. Serve cold.

Tender Cooked Cauliflower

Another good vegetable is cauliflower, which is cooked by steaming after washing and cutting away any dark spots. Put in steaming pot, and steam covered for 30 to 40 minutes, or until tender. You may have to add water.

Serve with melted butter, or better yet, *my wonderful cheese sauce.*

Richard's Cheese Sauce

For a good cheese sauce, buy a pound of American cheese from the deli (Velveeta is salty). Melt the cheese in a double boiler with ½ cup half & half, a tablespoon Worcestershire sauce, and a little fresh ground pepper or a few drops Tabasco. If you want a very mild sauce, then cut the Worcestershire to one teaspoon and skip the pepper or Tabasco.

Carrot Jell-o Salad

Carrot Jell-o salad is made by skinning and grating 4 or 5 carrots and adding to orange Jell-o. Variations can be to add a small can crushed pineapple (tuna can size) or a cup cottage cheese, or ¼ cup chopped pecans, or walnuts or all of the above.

> Hint: If you want a Jell-o mold to come out easily, then wipe the mold with mayonnaise before filling.

Oven Roastin' Corn

I have never had good luck roasting corn over coals or on a gas grill; it seems to burn on one side and not be cooked on the other, so I recommend roasting on the center rack of a 400° oven. Husk and clean the corn, and wrap in foil with about 2 teaspoons margarine on each ear. Bake for about 25 minutes; open carefully, so as not to spill the juice.

For boiled corn on the cob, you should husk and clean the corn and drop in a large pot of boiling water, to which you add about ¼ cup milk (No Salt). Bring back to a boil for about 5 minutes; then remove from burner. You can leave the corn in the hot water for 10 or 15 minutes, but not much longer or the corn will get tough. Serve the corn with lots of butter, salt and pepper.

Alabama Corn Patties

Try these corn patties. Scrape or grate the corn from the cob to make a cup of kernels. Combine with ¼ cup flour, 1 beaten egg, salt and fresh ground pepper. Shape into small patties (about 3") and brown in margarine in skillet.

These are also good for breakfast — with butter and maple syrup over them.

Escalloped Corn

3 tablespoons margarine
1 banana pepper
1 small onion, finely chopped
3 tablespoons flour
1 teaspoon salt
¼ teaspoon paprika
¼ teaspoon dry mustard
a pinch cayenne pepper
1 cup milk
2 cups fresh cut or canned whole kernel corn
one egg yolk
½ cup bread crumbs - optional

Escalloped corn starts with 3 tablespoons margarine in a skillet with a finely chopped small onion and a finely chopped banana pepper, cooked until tender. Add flour, salt, paprika, dry mustard and a pinch of cayenne. Stir until smooth. Then stir in milk and bring to boil, stirring constantly. Remove from heat, and add corn mixed with egg yolk. Turn mixture into a buttered pyrex dish and bake for 25 minutes at 400°.

You can sprinkle about ½ cup bread crumbs on the top before baking, if you like a little crust on the top.

Pecan Pie etc., etc.

Old Fashioned Pecan

For a great pecan pie, prepare a 9 inch unbaked pie shell; and preheat oven to 375°. In a large mixing bowl, mix 3 eggs, ¾ cup sugar, ⅛ teaspoon salt, & 1 cup dark corn syrup. Beat well and add 1 teaspoon vanilla and 1 cup pecan pieces. Pour into pie shell and bake 45 minutes. Now this is the basic pecan pie.

Getting Creative

But lets change it to use 1 tablespoon Amaretto instead of the vanilla; you will love it.

Like chocolate? Then melt 2 squares unsweetened chocolate with 3 tablespoons butter in double boiler - keeping water just to simmer - and cool the mixture about 5 minutes. Beat it into the corn syrup mixture, and you have a great chocolate pecan pie.

Also you can add 1 teaspoon cinnamon and ½ teaspoon nutmeg, which is what I like best in a walnut pie.

If you like walnuts, then make this pie with walnut pieces, but use *light* corn syrup (not dark).

VI

I really hope you are enjoying reading this book and talking about foods with your family and friends. Because so much of the news today is sad or bad, cooking is a great topic to keep things light and get everyone in a happy mood.

I guess that is what is really meant by "Soul Food." It makes the soul in us come alive in a joyful manner, and it makes it easier to be happy and to make others happy.

I remember once when I was invited to eat with some children in one of the cottages at the Masonic Home & School; and I watched this sweet child break lettuce into a bowl and begin to take the pieces in her hands and squeeze the lettuce. When I asked what she was doing, she said that there was no salad dressing, so she was making "Squeeze Salad." After squeezing the lettuce, she added salt and pepper and that was *Squeeze Salad*. God bless these children who are not only happy with what they have, but who are happy in sharing it.

Now . . . . to share some more delicious soul food recipes with you.

Kentucky Cheese Torte

1 pie crust, unbaked for 9" springform pan
½ cup ham, chopped fine
½ cup fresh grated Parmesan cheese
½ pound cream cheese
2 eggs
2 tablespoons milk
1½ cup spaghetti sauce

Butter springform, and press crust into pan and up sides to form shell. Bake about 5 minutes at 325° to set shell. Meanwhile, beat cream cheese until smooth. Then beat in Parmesan, eggs, & milk.

Spread ham on pie crust and pour cheese mixture over. Bake at 325° for about 1 hour. Then pour half of the spaghetti sauce over top and bake another 15 minutes. Cut into 6 or 8 slices and serve with a little sauce over the top. With a salad this will be a complete meal, as this is very rich.

Speaking of rich ....
Fudge Pie

one 9" unbaked pie crust in pyrex pie pan
½ cup margarine
3 eggs
¾ cup dark brown sugar
12 ounce pkg. semisweet chocolate morsels, melted
1 tablespoon Grand Marnier
½ cup flour
1 cup chopped pecans
Whipped cream topping

Cream margarine and slowly add sugar. Beat until light and fluffy; add eggs, one at a time; add melted chocolate morsels and Grand Marnier, and mix well. Stir in flour and nuts. Pour into pie shell and bake 25 minutes at 375°.

Let the pie cool on drainboard, and then chill in refrigerator at least 2 hours before serving with whipped cream topping.

Nutty-Cheese Toast

Here is a great toast for soups and salads.

Cut long French bread slices diagonally and brush both sides with olive oil (or about ½ cup margarine). Broil both sides about 30 seconds.

In a food processor with metal blade, process ½ cup fresh grated Parmesan cheese with ½ cup pecans, walnuts or almonds. When well blended, add ¼ cup olive oil and blend till smooth.

Spread mixture on bread and top with a little grated cheese and perhaps a few chopped nuts and broil till the cheese begins to melt (about 30-45 seconds).

Of course you can make these without the nuts.

Plan your work and work your plan.

Mississippi Stir Fry Beef w/Greens

Since this is a quick preparation item, get your items ready, using small bowls or plates to prepare the ingredients so that all will be at hand.

First, you'll need to:

>Mince a clove of garlic
>Chop a jalapeno pepper
>Make ½ cup bullion (use 1 cube in ½ cup hot water)
>Measure ¼ cup soy sauce
>Cut 1 pound flank steak into fairly thin strips

Mix garlic, jalapeno pepper, and soy sauce, with ¼ cup of bullion (save remaining ¼ cup for cornstarch). Pour this mixture over the flank steak strips.

See that the mixture covers well and let marinate while you:

>Begin cooking brown rice or egg noodles
>Grate two carrots
>Wash a pound of greens
>Measure 1 & ½ tablespoons cornstarch and mix with ¼ cup bullion
>Chop enough fresh cilantro for ¼ cup

Set aside each of these ingredients in separate containers.

Then, heat about a tablespoon of olive oil in wok or large deep skillet to medium high. Remove meat from marinade and sear quickly in pan (maybe two minutes) and remove from pan.

Add another tablespoon of olive oil; and when it is hot, add carrots and cook 3 to 4 minutes. Then add greens and cook till they start to wilt (about two minutes). Add the marinade and the cornstarch mixture.

Stir fry well until sauce starts to thicken, which will only be a minute or two. Sprinkle on cilantro, and serve with rice or buttered egg noodles.

And now you have a recipe that calls for greens, and can serve it to people who don't think they like greens. Of course you could use spinach if you can't find greens, but try the greens if you can get them.

Jarlsberg Cheese Fondue

Try this easy Jarlsberg cheese fondue.

Grate one pound Jarlsberg and mix with 2 tablespoons flour and ¼ teaspoon fresh ground nutmeg. Set aside.

Use a crock type fondue dish or a Corningware dish (at least 2 quart). Put in 1½ cups dry white wine and a minced clove of garlic. Microwave at full power for 4 to 5 minutes, until it is at the boiling point.

Put the cheese in a food processor with a metal blade; and after removing the garlic from the wine, add it through the top slowly with the processor running. After all wine has been added, process until smooth (approximately one minute).

Return the mixture to the fondue dish and heat in microwave about a minute.

Then whisk to smooth, and serve with a little chopped cilantro sprinkled on top.

Cream Puff Ring

Combine ½ cup butter, 1 cup water, ½ teaspoon salt, and 1 teaspoon sugar in 2 quart sauce pan. Heat until butter melts and remove from heat. Stir in 1 cup of flour and keep stirring until the mixture is smooth and comes away from sides of pan. Next, mix in 4 eggs, one at a time.

Drop the dough mixture by spoonful (making a 9 inch circle) onto a greased baking sheet. Smooth out the circle with the back of a spoon, which has been moistened with water.

Brush top with beaten egg (diluted with a tablespoon water) and bake in preheated 400° oven for 40-45 minutes until golden brown and crisp. Let puff cool completely before slicing. Remove any soft dough and fill with cooked Jell-o vanilla pudding and sprinkle powdered sugar on top.

To vary filling, you can use fresh strawberries, peaches, or other fruit.

You can use whipped cream instead of pudding. You will need to whip about 1 & ½ cups whipping cream. Flavor with Chambroud or other liqueur.

Make an icing of 2½ tablespoons boiling water, mixed with a cup powdered sugar. Flavor icing by mixing a teaspoon of instant coffee with the boiling water.

By the way, you can make mocha whipped cream by using 2 teaspoons instant coffee in 2 teaspoons boiling water. Dissolve well. Let this cool, and add 2 tablespoons cocoa and a teaspoon of vanilla.

You can also use ¼ cup toasted almonds sprinkled on the powdered sugar icing. Now use the basic recipe and do your own thing, as this is a great desert.

Still Hungry?

Oatmeal Pound Cake

Process 1 cup oatmeal in food processor for about 2 minutes. Then add 1¾ cups flour, 1 teaspoon baking powder and ½ teaspoon salt.

In large mixing bowl, combine 1¼ cups sugar, and two sticks butter or margarine, and mix until fluffy. Then add 3 eggs and the grated rind of a large lemon and mix well.

Next, add the flour & oat mixture and ¾ cup of milk, a little of each at a time, mixing until blended well. Pour into a 9x5 loaf pan, prepared with Bakers Joy, and bake 1¼ hours at 325°.

Test with broom straw or toothpick. When it comes out clean, cool about 15 minutes in pan and then turn out on plate. Cool completely, and sprinkle with powdered sugar.

Or you can make an icing of the juice of the lemon you have previously grated the rind off of. Mix juice with a 4 ounce package of cream cheese and a tablespoon of powdered sugar

Note: If you use this icing, you should keep the cake in the refrigerator.

Variation:

For a great topping, which looks fancy but is really easy, thaw a 10 or 12 ounce package of frozen strawberries or raspberries and put about ⅓ third of the berries aside (without the juice). Put the remaining berries and juice in blender and blend smooth. Spoon over slices, and put the reserved whole berries on top.

Warning: *If you are making this for a certain meal, you better tell the family to stay away, because this is a wonderful cake to "just swipe a quick slice of " as you pass through the kitchen. But remember that those sticky fingers belong to the ones you are cooking for. Isn't it great to please them with food you prepared with love?*

A Great Dinner:

Orange Vinaigrette

Orange Vinaigrette is made in a quart jar. Mix ¾ cup orange juice, 1 cup red wine vinegar, 1 & ¾ cup olive oil, 1 teaspoon salt and 1 teaspoon fresh ground pepper. Shake until salt is dissolved and let it sit a half day at room temperature. Then refrigerate and shake periodically until you are ready to use it.

My Orange Vinaigrette Salad

Here is the salad I love with the vinaigrette. On a bed of bib or leaf lettuce, arrange pickled beets and mandarin orange slices. Spoon on the vinaigrette and decorate with a ring of red onion.

Pepper Beef Tenderloin

Beef tenderloin is fantastic this way. First in a food processor, grind together 2 tablespoons peppercorns and a tablespoon of coriander seeds (leave coarse). Mix in a teaspoon salt and turn onto a board or wax paper so you can roll the meat in the mix.

Rub the meat with about a teaspoon olive oil, and then roll the tenderloin in the mix until it is well coated.

Coat the bottom of a roasting pan with about a tablespoon of olive oil. Place meat in pan and cook at 425° for 30 to 35 minutes. Let meat stand 5 minutes or so before slicing. The meat should be medium to medium rare, so you can adjust cooking about 5 minutes either way, as you like.

If you have two ovens, you can make these *baked potatoes* with this roast.

Wash and fork potatoes and wrap each potato with a slice of bacon and then with foil. Bake at 400° for about an hour. Test with a fork. When the fork can go all the way through, potatoes are done.

Serve baked potatoes with:

> *Sunflower seeds*
> *Poppy Seeds*
> *Butter*
> *Sour cream*
> *Heavy Cream*
> *Raisins*
> *Chopped crisp bacon*
> *Chopped green onion tops*
> *Cheddar or other cheese*

Smothered Baked Potatoes

In lieu of the tenderloin, you can make the potatoes a meal by topping with chili, bar-b-q, Italian meat sauce, etc.

If your potatoes are done before serving time, then you should keep the oven warm. When you add the toppings, put the potatoes on a cookie sheet and return to the oven for 3 - 4 minutes to get them good and hot.

VII

Is it Snack Time?

Shortbread Cookies

Shortbread cookies are not only good for an afternoon snack, but they go fast. They are not too sweet and seem to enhance the flavor of hot tea. The oatmeal gives them a nutty taste.

Combine 2 cups oatmeal with 1¼ cups flour and set aside.

Beat together (until fluffy):

> *½ pound butter or margarine (not light)**
> *½ cup sugar*
> *1 teaspoon vanilla*

* (If you are going to use margarine, make sure it is not the light type in that the way they seem to make something "light" is to put a lot of water in it.)

Blend in oats & flour and pat out the shortbread on an ungreased cookie sheet. Use a fork to mark off where you will break these cookies or cut in strips or other shapes. The dough should be about ⅛ inch thick.

Bake at 350° about 18 minutes. Cool about five to six minutes, and sprinkle with powdered sugar. Then remove from tray to cool completely on wire rack (if you don't have a wire rack - get one - but in the mean time you can use a clean terry towel on the drain board).

For variation, use ¼ teaspoon almond extract and cut vanilla to ½ teaspoon. Then press a few slivered almonds into top of cookies before baking - use slivered almonds (not flakes, because flakes get too brown.)

Old Fashioned Sand Tarts

For sand tarts, beat together 2 sticks of butter, ¾ cup powdered sugar, and 2 teaspoons vanilla, until fluffy. Add in 2 cups flour and ¼ teaspoon salt; mix until well blended. Stir in ¾ cup chopped pecans.

Shape into crescents and bake at 325° for about 15 minutes. Tops will be light. Bottoms will get golden brown, but do not let bottoms get too brown.

Dust the cookies with powdered sugar while still warm.

For variation, use ½ teaspoon almond extract; cut vanilla to 1 teaspoon. In a food processor with a metal blade, grind ½ cup oatmeal until it is coarse. Remove to small bowl and grind ¾ cup almonds until coarse - take it easy with almonds in order not to grind too fine. Add to cookies and omit pecans; shape and bake as above.

Potato Pancakes

For potato pancakes you will need:

1 large, or 2 medium, or 3 small potatoes — skinned and grated
1 medium onion, grated
1 large egg
3 tablespoons flour
salt and fresh ground pepper to taste

Stir all together and fry by spoonfuls in hot oil — 3 to 4 minutes per side. Drain on paper towel.

German style is to serve with sour cream and applesauce.

Penuche

To make this wonderful candy, you'll need a candy thermometer.

Penuche is made by lining a square pyrex with plastic wrap.

In a sauce pan, combine 2 cups light brown sugar, ⅔ cup heavy cream, and ¼ teaspoon salt and stir over medium heat until the mixture comes to a boil. Let simmer about 30 minutes or until it reaches 240° on your thermometer.

Remove pan to trivet (the metal kind so air gets under bottom). Break up a tablespoon butter on top of candy - do not stir in until thermometer gets to 110°. Then add a teaspoon vanilla and beat with electric mixer until candy is very thick and loses its sheen —approximately 5 minutes.

Press into pyrex dish and refrigerate. Cut into squares when firm.

Bread Pudding

For bread pudding, spray a 9 x 5 pyrex dish with Pam.

In a mixing bowl, combine:
>2 egg yolks
>1 cup Pet milk
>1 cup whole milk (Not 2% or low-fat)
>1 teaspoon vanilla
>6 tablespoons sugar
>¼ teaspoon salt

Beat until sugar dissolves, and stir in 3 slices of stale light bread (if your bread is fresh, let it sit on drain board over night). If you like, add ½ cup plumped raisins and ¼ cup chopped pecans. Mix well, pour in pyrex dish, and bake at 400° for 20 to 25 minutes — don't let tops get too brown.

While the pudding cooks, beat the egg whites stiff with 2 tablespoons sugar and a pinch of salt. Spread on pudding and return to oven until golden brown, usually only 3 or 4 minutes.

Note: For baking I recommend Baker's Joy, but for frying and certain baked custards, you will need Pam, because you don't want the flour — just a non-stick surface.

How 'bout dinner?

When you don't feel like cooking, then try a bread & butter sandwich made from a fresh seeded bun and (if someone hasn't eaten them all) cold sweet hot pork-n-beans with dip size Fritos to scoop them up. Now that is what I just had for dinner with a good glass of Iced Tea.

Chicken Fried Steak

If you want a little meat, try tenderized pork cutlets which will be more tender than beef or chicken. You can usually get a package of two, which is a meal (maybe for two).

Unwrap and place in small bowl with some milk. Put flour in a flat tray and season with Lawry's salt and pepper. Take cutlets from milk and coat with flour and fry in olive oil. This is quick and easy.

Of course this is the same recipe for either beef or chicken. For best results, be sure to get the butcher to run the meat through the tenderizer.

Richard's Chili

I have already said that Wick Fowler's Two Alarm Chili Mix makes good chili and is easy; but here is my scratch recipe without tomatoes. Not only is it relatively easy to fix, but it's terrific to eat.

3 pounds ground beef (Regular not extra lean)
3 garlic cloves
6 tablespoons chili powder
2 teaspoons ground cumin
1 teaspoon oregano
3 tablespoons flour
6 beef bullion cubes
1 large onion

Brown ground beef in a large deep skillet; crumble well. Reduce heat, and add finely minced garlic cloves, chili power, ground cumin, oregano, and flour. Stir well to coat all the meat. Add 2 cups hot water with 4 beef bullion cubes melted in it. Simmer for about 2 hours, stirring occasionally.

After the chili has simmered for about an hour, add another cup of water with 2 bullion cubes, and add a grated or finely chopped onion. During the last half hour, keep watching so that the chili does not stick as it starts to thicken. You may have to reduce heat and cook an extra half hour. Slow cooking is what will make the meat tender and the chili flavorful.

Turn off the stove, and let the chili cool. Refrigerate over night in order to (1) tighten the flavor and (2) harden the grease so you can lift it off the top.

You can freeze part of this for up to three months.

For those who want it hot, add some Tabasco; or you can mix ¼ to ½ teaspoon red cayenne pepper with the chili powder.

I suggest you try serving this with 1 cup chili:

½ cup whole kernel corn and two cups cooked brown rice...yummy!

And speaking of yummy ...

After School Muffins

For not only a good but nutritious after school snack, try these apple muffins.

In a large mixing bowl, beat together:

⅔ cup apple juice
½ cup vegetable oil (olive oil is too heavy)
1½ teaspoons vanilla
1 egg

Then mix in:

2 cups flour
¼ cup brown sugar
¼ cup white sugar
1 tablespoon baking powder
½ teaspoon salt

Mix only to moisten flour, because you want the batter lumpy. Stir in 1½ cups finely chopped apple; and bake about 20 minutes at 400° in muffin pan, prepared with Bakers Joy.

For variation, you could add ½ cup chopped walnuts or pecans, ½ cup oat meal (raw), or use cranapple instead of apple juice. Or reduce chopped apple to one cup and use ½ cup chopped plumped raisins, or ½ cup cranberries (To prepare cranberries, chop fresh cranberries and put in boiling water for about a minute; drain and use when cool).

If you really want to get fancy and make the muffins especially good, sprinkle some Kretschmer Honey Crunch Wheat Germ and a little brown sugar on top before baking. Let the muffins sit about 5 minutes before baking in order for the topping to absorb a little moisture.

I really hope you are thinking of the many ways that you can take the recipes here and vary them for you and your family. When you start adding your own touch is when you really start having fun cooking, and you can share your discovery with others.

I could never write enough additions and variations to each recipe to cover all of the possibilities; so I hope what you read here starts you to thinking.

Easy Tuna Casserole

I like tuna casserole, and it is easy. Just prepare a box of Noodle Roni and add a can of tuna and a cup of crushed potato chips.

You can also make this with a can of chicken (same size as the tuna and near it in the store). Note that I did not specify which flavor Noodle- Roni. That is so you can pick which one to try first and then try this dish with the other flavors. This is so quick and easy, and all you need is a salad for dinner.

Now if you are making it for a covered dish, then after you add the potato chips and tuna, turn it into a buttered casserole dish, top with cheese and pop in hot oven to melt cheese on top.

If you have some left over, pour ¼ cup milk and a tablespoon butter over the leftover portion and heat in oven at 350° until it is hot. You can add a little cheese if it is too soupy.

This is also something you can just keep adding things to — like:

½ cup chopped water chestnuts, ¼ cup chopped pimento, a small can of green peas, and/or corn. How about ¼ cup chopped green bell pepper and ¼ cup red bell (which you cook in butter before adding).

If using chicken, try mixing in ¼ cup chopped fresh cilantro.

POPCORN PUDDIN'

I know this sounds weird, but try it anyway — especially when teenagers are home; for they really like it.

Pop seven cups popcorn and remove the old maids (i.e. the unpopped kernels). In a mixing bowl, beat 2 tablespoons melted butter, 3 eggs, 1¼ cups half & half, and a teaspoon vanilla.

Beat until well blended, then add ¾ cup light brown sugar (firmly packed), a teaspoon cinnamon, ¼ teaspoon nutmeg and ¼ teaspoon salt. Stir well and add a large (30 ounce) can fruit cocktail,(drained).

Now add the popcorn and mix until the popcorn is well coated and it shrinks in size some. Spray a one quart microwave casserole dish with Pam; turn mixture into casserole, and microwave uncovered at full power for 15 minutes.

For variation, add 1 cup plumped raisins, and/or ½ cup chopped pecans, walnuts or almonds, or sprinkle wheat germ on top when cooking.

Music will soothe the savage beast, but a good pudding will make it cooperative.
— Phineas T. Strongtoe

Breadstick Snacks

This is a great snack for kids if you can keep the adults away from it. Get a package of sesame bread sticks — the kind that are about 6 inches long (use garlic, cheese, or plain. I like sesame best).

Put a package of thin or regular sliced bacon (not thick sliced) out on the drain until it reaches room temperature. Take a strip of bacon, stretch it out and wrap it so it spirals around the bread stick. Fold it around the ends so it all doesn't slide to the center when cooking. Place the breadsticks on a microwave bacon pan and microwave at ½ power for five minutes and then turn pan halfway around and microwave on full power another two minutes or until bacon is crisp. Let these cool at least 10 minutes, so they are good and crisp.

Maybe you'll need to buy two packages of bread sticks, so you will have some to eat too.

Gingerbread Cookies

For gingerbread cookies, you will want plumped raisins, candied orange and grapefruit or lemon rind, silver sugar or colored decorations and white icing (available in an aerosol can at the grocery store).

In a 1 quart bowl, sift together 2½ cups flour, ½ teaspoon baking soda, 1 teaspoon cinnamon, ½ teaspoon nutmeg, & ½ teaspoon salt.

Cream one stick unsalted butter with ½ firmly packed dark brown sugar. Then beat in ½ cup molasses and the grated rind of one orange; beat in one egg until smooth and gradually beat in dry ingredients until smooth.

Refrigerate until firm. Roll out about ⅛ inch thick, and cut into shapes.

Prepare baking sheet with Pam, and place cookies on sheet. Decorate with raisins, fruit, colored sugar (but not icing) and bake at 350° about 6 to 7 minutes — note: the tops will get firm but should not color.

After cookies cool, you can finish decorating with icing.

I can give you a six-word formula for success in cooking, or in life:

Think things through.
Then follow through.

VIII

COMES THE DAWN

*After a while you learn subtle differences
between holding a hand and sharing a life
and you learn that love doesn't mean possession
and company doesn't mean security
and loneliness is universal*

*And you learn that kisses aren't contracts
and presents aren't promises
and you begin to accept your defeats
with your head up and your eyes open
with the grace of an adult
not the grief of a child*

*And you learn to build your hopes on today
as the future has a way of falling apart
that tomorrow's ground is uncertain
and each step taken creates a path and direction
toward the promise of a brighter dawn*

*And you learn that even sunshine burns
if you get too much
so you plant your own garden
and nourish your own soil
instead of waiting for someone
to bring you flowers*

*And you learn that love, true love
always has joys and sorrows
seems ever present
yet is never quite the same
becoming more and less than love
so difficult to define*

*And you learn that through it all
you really can endure
that you really are strong
that you do have value*

*YOU LEARN AND GROW,
AND WITH EVERY GOODBYE*

YOU LEARN.

— Anonymous

COLE-N-SAK

One head cabbage
25 saltines
one egg
¼ pound butter

Select a head of cabbage with outer leaves that you can remove and reserve. Wash cabbage; and after removing eight to ten outer leaves, chop the cabbage and boil until tender in a large pot (12 quart). Drain the cabbage in a colander and mix with mashed crackers. Mix a beaten egg in with the cabbage. Add salt and pepper to taste, and blend well.

In a small bowl, place a flour sack or thin dish cloth and arrange the reserved leaves to form a head. Scoop the mixture into the cabbage leaves and put some leaves on top to form the head. Bring the flour sack up and tie it to keep the cabbage in a ball. Return the head to the pan of boiling water (be sure the cabbage is covered with water) and boil about 35 minutes.

While the cabbage is cooking, melt the butter over medium heat and cook until it just begins to brown; and remove from heat. Untie the cabbage and turn onto plate. The head will be firm, and you will slice it with a sharp knife and serve with the browned butter.

This is a wonderful dish to try on those who don't think they like cabbage. Who knows? You may change their minds.

I have such a wonderful memory of this dish and "Oma" whom I loved so very much.

ESCALLOPED PORK CHOPS

about 3 pounds pork chops or pork steak with bones removed
yellow mustard
6 medium red potatoes
1 large onion
2 to 3 cups milk
salt and pepper

In a 9 x 13 pyrex pan, line the bottom with a layer of potatoes, cut in circles (peeled or unpeeled). Spread a little mustard on one side of the pork, as if you were making a sandwich; and place that side down in the pan, making a layer with the meat. Sprinkle with salt and pepper, and put a layer of thin sliced onion on next. Then finish with another layer of potatoes. Pour milk over to cover the potatoes. Cover the pyrex with foil and bake at 325° for 1½ hours, periodically checking to make sure milk has not cooked away. Add more milk as necessary.

Rice Krispie Treats

¼ pound margarine
1 pound pkg. marshmallows
10 cups Rice Krispies

Melt margarine in deep skillet or pan. Add marshmallows and melt, stirring constantly. Add the Rice Krispies; mix well, and turn into a 9x13 buttered pyrex dish. You will need to butter your fingers so you can press the mixture down. Let cool and cut into squares. Store in air tight container.

*A good dinner sharpens wit,
while it softens the heart.*
John Doran

South Texas Pork Stew

*3 pounds boneless pork cut into 1" cubes
3 cups water
¼ cup oil
3 chicken bullion cubes
1 large onion
2 fresh hot chilies
2 fresh banana peppers
2 red bell peppers
½ cup chili powder
2 tablespoons cumin
¼ teaspoon cayenne pepper
1 teaspoon Salt*

Mix the pork, chili powder, cumin, cayenne and salt; and set aside.

Chop onion, and cut peppers into strips. Simmer in stew pot for about 15 minutes until soft. Add pork mixture, water, and bullion cubes; and bring to a boil. Reduce heat to simmer for about 1½ hours; put cover on for the first hour, and then remove to let the sauce thicken the last 30 minutes.

This is great served over brown rice.

Dallas Jambalaya

½ *pound thin sliced pepperoni*
2 pounds peeled & deveined shrimp
4 onions, chopped
1 cup chopped celery
2 red & 2 green bell peppers, chopped
4 cloves garlic
⅓ cup oil
a large can tomatoes (30 ounce)
1 teaspoon each cayenne, oregano, thyme, salt
½ teaspoon black pepper
2½ cups raw white rice
5 chicken bullion cubes

Cut pepperoni slices into quarters. Then in a large dutch oven, heat oil; and add onion, celery, and minced garlic. Simmer about 10 minutes. Add pepperoni, and cook about 10 minutes longer. Drain tomatoes - reserve juice - and mash up tomatoes before adding to the mixture. Then add juice and enough water to make a total of five cups liquid. Add rice and bullion cubes, and bring to boil.

Cover and reduce heat to simmer for about 30 to 35 minutes — until the rice is just done. Add shrimp, and cook about 3 or 4 minutes. Remove from heat and let sit uncovered for 2 to 3 minutes to tighten.

Serve with a salad and crusty french bread.

For a salad, I suggest lettuce and tomatoes with fresh basil and a light vinegar & oil dressing.

Italian Sausage Sauce

1½ pounds Italian sweet sausage
4 onions
4 green bell peppers
4 minced cloves of garlic
¼ cup olive oil
½ teaspoon each oregano, salt and pepper
2 large cans tomatoes

In a large deep frying pan or stew pot, brown sausage and remove. Add oil, chopped onions and peppers, and garlic to the pan. Simmer until clear (about 10 minutes). Then stir in sausage, tomatoes, salt, pepper, and oregano; and bring to a boil. Reduce heat and simmer for about 20 minutes or until the sauce begins to thicken.

This should be enough sauce for about a pound of spaghetti.

You can completely change this sauce by using 1½ pounds ground lean beef or ground chicken.

Note: If you use ground chicken, cook lightly with some oil but do not brown or chicken will get tough.
Cook ground beef or chicken with oil in order that the meat will blend in with the sauce and not lump up.

Easy Salmon Patties

1 can salmon
¼ cup finely chopped or grated onion
1 egg
15 saltines, finely crushed
oil for frying

Combine salmon, onion, egg, and crackers in bowl. Mix well and shape into patties. Fry about 3 minutes on each side or until light brown. Serve with *Spicy Caper Mayonnaise.*

Spicy Caper Mayonnaise

1 cup mayonnaise
1 tablespoon chopped capers
Dash Tabasco
½ teaspoon Dijon mustard

Combine ingredients and let sit for 20 minutes to tighten flavor.

These salmon patties are an easy meal with Chicken Rice-a-Roni and English peas heated with butter and fresh pepper.

What do you do with left over chicken planks, french fries, and onion rings?

Cut them up and mix together with a can of Franco-American chicken gravy. Put in buttered baking dish. Cover with Swiss cheese, and bake at 300° for about 20 minutes, or until bubbling; do not brown.

(If you have only fries & chicken, then chop ½ onion and cook in a tablespoon of margarine until clear, and mix with fries & chicken as above).

WASTE NOT - WANT NOT

Nuked Zucchini

Cut the ends from a medium size zucchini, and split lengthwise by cutting a line down the center (but not through). Place on microwave dish, and cook on high for three minutes. Turn the dish half way around, and spread a small amount of butter on top of squash.

Nuke on high for another three minutes, and check for doneness. Microwave one or two more minutes, as desired; and sprinkle on a little veggi-sal and fresh ground pepper. It is ready to eat.

You might also sprinkle *very lightly* a little nutmeg for a special flavor.

See how easy it is to show your love with food. What a great feeling to prepare something for someone you care about and see them enjoy what YOU have done for them.

I also have a great feeling as I share with you the things that I have learned about cooking. I truly hope that you get as much joy from using this book as I have in writing it.

IX

Dorothy's Hummingbird Cake

3 cups flour
1 teaspoon baking soda
1 teaspoon cinnamon
½ teaspoon salt
2 cups sugar
3 beaten eggs
¾ cup oil (just not olive),
2 cups mashed, over ripe bananas
8 ounce can crushed pineapple w/juice
1 cup chopped walnuts or pecans
1 ½ teaspoons vanilla

Combine flour, soda, cinnamon, salt, & sugar in large mixing bowl. Add oil to beaten eggs and stir into flour until just moistened. Stir in bananas, pineapple, nuts, & vanilla. Do not beat.

Pour batter into three 9"round pans, sprayed with Baker's Joy, and bake at 350° for about 25 minutes. Cool in pans about 8 to 10 minutes. Remove to wire rack to cool completely.

Frost with *Cream Cheese Frosting.*

Cream Cheese Frosting

8 ounce package cream cheese
½ cup BUTTER
1 teaspoon vanilla
1 pound powdered sugar

Cream together butter and cream cheese and slowly add powdered sugar; stir in vanilla and beat until light and fluffy. Ice the cake and sprinkle coconut or nuts on top.

Coco - Loco Pound Cake

½ cup unsalted butter
½ cup Crisco
8 ounce package cream cheese
3 cups flour
3 cups sugar
6 large eggs
¼ teaspoon baking soda
¼ teaspoon salt
1 teaspoon vanilla
1 tablespoon Coco-Loco Coconut Drink Mix
8 oz fresh shaved coconut
(or packaged, if you have to.)

Sift together flour, baking soda, and salt; and set aside.

Then cream butter, shortening, and cream cheese — beat it well. Beat in sugar, a little at a time; and then add eggs, one at a time, beating after each egg.

Add vanilla & Coco-Loco; then stir in flour and coconut. Mix just until blended. Pour into 10" tube pan, prepared with Baker's Joy. Bake at 325° for 1 & ½ hours Cool about 10 minutes before turning out of pan onto a wire rack. Coco-Loco is the milky stuff you get to make Pina-Coladas; so if you use another brand, it is O.K.

Note: To test if a cake is done, take a straw from your broom. Take it from the top where it is bound to the handle. Cut it so it is straight and push into cake. If it comes out clean; the cake is done.

Do not try to reuse as straw, as it gets oily from a use and will not give a correct reading on second use. I use a broom straw in that a toothpick is sometimes too short.

POT D'CREME — EGG CUSTARD — FLAN' ETC...

This custard is truly an international dessert. I will not get into who it really belongs to, but from an American stand point, we can just enjoy it.

You will need:

four 10 oz custard cups (which you can get in Corningware)
a 9 x 13 pyrex
½ cup sugar
another ⅓ cup sugar
3 eggs
2 cups milk
½ teaspoon vanilla
ground nutmeg (fresh ground is best)

Cook the ½ cup sugar in a small cast iron skillet until it turns golden - keep on medium heat and stir constantly. Pour this syrup into the four custard cups.

Beat together the eggs, sugar, vanilla, and a pinch of nutmeg. Slowly add the milk, beating well. Divide custard into the four cups.

This part is sometimes tricky, so here is how I do it.

Position oven rack at about center level. Slide out the oven rack far enough to set the pyrex on it. Place the custard cups in pyrex.

I heat water in a teapot on the stove and carefully pour hot water in the pyrex to about an inch or half way on the cups.

Next cover the pyrex with foil and gently slide the rack into the oven, being careful not to slosh the water into the custard. Bake at 350° for about 45 minutes.

Test custard with a table knife inserted in the center. When custard is done, lift out of water and cool for about 10 minutes.

Then loosen edge with knife around top and invert onto small plate to serve.

Note: I have had no luck at trying to double this recipe, but you can use 6 to 8 oz custard cups and it will cook in about 40 minutes.

CHICKEN PIE ESPECIAL

4 cups cooked chicken chunks
½ lb regular ground sausage cooked, crumbled, & drained
1 cup sliced fresh mushrooms, sauteed in butter
1 can cooked peas & carrots
2 small white onions chopped and sauteed in butter
pie crust for a two crust 9" pie
6 tablespoons of both butter and flour
2 cups chicken stock
1 cup whipping cream
½ teaspoon fresh ground pepper
1 teaspoon salt.

Melt the butter in a heavy skillet and add flour. Stir for 2 minutes and then slowly add chicken stock, cream, salt, and pepper. Cook about 5 to 6 minutes, stirring to keep smooth until sauce begins to thicken. Remove from heat and mix in chicken, mushrooms, onion, and sausage.

Line a deep casserole dish with pie crust and fill with mixture. Put on top crust and cut slits so the steam can escape. Crimp edges and trim off excess. Bake at 425° for 25 to 30 minutes. Start watching close at 20 minutes to see that the crust doesn't get too brown.

> *A soul without watchfulness is, like a city without walls, exposed to the inroads of all its enemies.*
> — Thomas Secker

Cheesie Chicken Casserole

6 boneless chicken breasts
6 slices swiss cheese
1 can cream of chicken soup
¼ cup milk
1 package Stove Top Stuffing
¼ cup melted margarine

Butter bottom of a 9 x 13 pyrex baking dish and place chicken breasts on bottom. Cover with Swiss cheese. Mix together soup and milk, and pour over cheese. Sprinkle Stove Top evenly over the dish, and pour margarine over the top.

Cover with foil and bake at 325° for 50 minutes. Remove foil and bake 5 to 10 minutes longer, watching to see it doesn't get too brown or start to dry out. (Have a chicken bullion cube dissolved in cup of hot water ready to pour over — use only what you need to keep moist).

Sweet Potato Pie

1 lb can mashed sweet potatoes
1 cup Pet milk
2 Eggs
¾ cup sugar
2 teaspoon vanilla
¼ teaspoon almond extract
a 9" single pie crust in a pyrex pie pan

Bake pie crust for 10 minutes in 325° oven. Combine all other ingredients; pour into baked pie shell, and bake for 35 minutes longer or until center is set (table knife comes out clean). Let cool on drain board, and serve with whipped topping.

Whipped Cream

Whip 1 cup whipping cream until it thickens; stir in ½ cup powdered sugar and whip until it forms peaks — stop — do not over whip.

Pumpkin Pie

Use pumpkin instead of sweet potatoes in the above recipe. Add ½ teaspoon cinnamon.

For variation, both of these pies can have ½ cup chopped pecans or walnuts, and/or ½ cup fresh grated coconut or toasted coconut.

Great Northern Beans

2 cups Beans
1 cup thin sliced carrots
1 cup thin sliced celery
½ teaspoon Veggi Sal
½ teaspoon cracked pepper

Wash beans, and add all ingredients to a 3 quart saucepan with about 2 quarts of water. Cook at medium low until beans are tender — about 2 hours.

Spiced Sauerkraut w/ Canadian Bacon

Fresh sauerkraut is hard to find, but search and you will be well rewarded for your trouble; for this will introduce you to a very special dish.

2 pounds fresh sauerkraut
1 tablespoon olive oil
1 onion, very finely chopped
1 tablespoon light brown sugar
½ pound Canadian bacon cut in four thick slices
2 cups water
1 large peeled potato.

In a cheese cloth bag place:
1 stick cinnamon
6 whole black peppercorns
¼ teaspoon caraway seeds
3 bay leaves
2 whole allspice and 5 whole juniper berries.

First, wash the sauerkraut in a colander under cold water. Place in large bowl of cold water; set aside for 30 minutes. Remove from water, a little at a time; and press to dry. Place on cutting board; pat with a paper towel to complete drying. In a 4 quart casserole (one with a well fitting lid), heat oil; add onion, and cook until light brown. Remove from heat. Add sauerkraut, sugar, and 2 cups of fresh water to the casserole; mix. Push the spices in their bag down into kraut, and place bacon over the top. Bring to boil at medium high heat; reduce heat to very low, and simmer for 30 minutes. Grate potato over kraut, and gently mix it in. Place lid on the kraut casserole, and cook for 2 hours over low heat. Serve with *Great Northern Beans* and Pumpernickel rolls or bread and unsalted butter for a complete German meal.

X

Tips on Flavored Steamed Veggies

Fresh ginger is usually sold in bulk by the pound. Break off a fat thick piece — no more than two ounces, for this goes a long way.

To steam cook veggies, which seems to be very popular these days, you need a large pan and a steamer insert (which looks like a colander with sides that fold to fit the pan and legs to keep it out of the water). When steaming, watch to see you don't boil the water away. Keep a teapot of hot water, so you don't put cold water into your steamer.

Now about the ginger, grate about ¼ teaspoon into the water and it will flavor the steam, but use very little. You might also try a stick of cinnamon in the water. Or ONE whole clove, and I mean only one . . .

24 Hour Icebox Salad

In a large deep bowl, put the following in layers:

3 cups shredded lettuce
1 cup sliced carrots (slice as thin coins)
1 cup sliced Zucchini squash (raw)
1 cup shredded red cabbage
4 cups cooked macaroni shells
3 sliced hard boiled eggs
a small red onion thinly sliced and spread in rings
1 cup julienne of ham
1 box frozen english peas (thawed & drained)
½ cup grated Cheddar cheese
½ cup grated Jarlsburg cheese

Over the top, spread the special dressing (below); cover bowl with saran wrap, and refrigerate overnight. Sprinkle seasoned croutons on top and serve.

Note: You can make this in the morning, but it needs to chill at least 8 hours in the refrigerator.

Richard's Special Dressing

Combine the following:

1 cup mayonnaise
½ cup sour cream
¼ cup milk
2 teaspoons Dijon mustard
1 teaspoon sugar
¼ teaspoon salt
fresh ground pepper.

Mix Well.

I suggest you serve with a bowl of croutons on the side so that everyone gets some.

And if it is summer and the season is right for avocado, then garnish the top with slices of avocado at serving time.

This is a super party salad, and makes a great covered dish item; for it is prepared well in advance.

On top of the ham layer, you can add a cup of chopped bell pepper and a layer of sliced cucumber, if you desire.

Cranberry Relish

4 cups fresh cranberries
2 large apples — peeled, cored, and chopped
½ cup yellow raisins
The pulp sections cut from two large oranges
½ cup orange juice
2 cups sugar
1 teaspoon cinnamon,
½ teaspoon powdered ginger
1 tablespoon vinegar

Combine all in large saucepan, and bring to a medium boil. Cook until the liquid is a thin syrup, boiling about 20 minutes. Let cool some before putting in a bottle and refrigerating over night.

Hints: Use a very sharp thin knife to cut out the orange. Also, I sometimes like to grate with a fine grater the rind of one orange to make about 2 tablespoons.

Also change the sugar to 1½ cups white and ½ dark cup brown. Omit the vinegar and use dry white wine.

Serve this for lunch with a cold roast pork and a lettuce and tomato salad with a wonderful ...

Fresh Basil, Vinegar & Oil Dressing

½ cup olive oil
1 cup cider vinegar
a "Bunch" of fresh basil leaves — washed and patted dry

Mix together and let sit for at least a couple of hours.

Mouth Watering Pot Roast

This is a great roast, although I love the veggies and the gravy even more than the meat.

To make good gravy, get a fairly FAT roast (Not too lean). The size of the roast will depend on how many you want to feed or how much you want left over. The following will feed four with some left over.

3 pound roast (chuck, blade, or rump, although I like chuck best)
1 pound carrots
3 large yellow onions
4 to 5 stalks celery
3 pounds red or white potatoes
1 package McCormick Pot Roast Seasoning

Put roast on rack; and put onions, celery, and carrots around the roast. Pour on one cup water, and sprinkle roast seasoning over both roast and veggies. Cover your roasting pan, and cook 4 hours at 225°. Put in potatoes, and cook about 2 hours longer. Watch after about 1½ hours to see that you have plenty of liquid; add water if necessary.

This is great with the natural gravy, but if you like a thick brown gravy, then brown ½ cup flour in a heavy skillet. This is done by heating skillet over medium high and stirring flour in DRY skillet until it is golden. Add 3 tablespoons margarine and mix well. Then add the natural gravy from the roast and thin with water as required. Note that this may need some salt.

Delicious Artichokes

Select artichokes with closed buds and without brown spots. Cut stems so that chokes are able to sit upright.

Place steamer rack in pan and add water until it is just to the bottom of the rack. Place chokes on rack, stems down, and bring water to boil. Squeeze a little lemon juice over each choke. Then cover pot and reduce heat to let water simmer for 45 to 50 minutes, keeping an eye on the water. The chokes will have changed color when they are done.

Lift out chokes with tongs and serve with melted butter, garlic butter, mayonnaise, curry mayonnaise, etc. Serve hot or cold.

Sweet Corn Relish

20 ears fresh corn
1 bunch celery
1 small cabbage
5 white onions
2 red bell peppers
2 banana peppers
1 quart white vinegar
2 cups sugar
1 cup flour
1/3 cup salt
1 teaspoon dry mustard
1/2 teaspoon turmeric
1/2 teaspoon cayenne
1/4 teaspoon ground clove

Cut corn from ears; chop celery, onions, and cabbage; and put in large pot.

Mix flour with a little of the vinegar, and add more vinegar until it is all mixed. Then add sugar and seasonings, and stir well. Pour over corn in pot, and bring to a boil. Reduce heat to simmer for about 45 to 50 minutes. Let cool for about 5 minutes; then put in glass jars and seal.

The turnpike to most people's hearts, I find, lies through their mouths, or I mistake mankind.
—John Wolcot

Green Bean Bundles

I'm giving this recipe with 2 cans "Del Monte Whole Green Beans", but you may want to double this; for both kids and adults eat these like nothing you have ever seen.

They are so easy too....
>2 cans whole green beans
>1 pound regular sliced bacon
>Garlic salt
>⅓ cup melted margarine
>½ cup dark brown sugar
>Toothpicks

In a small pyrex dish, melt margarine in microwave on high for about 30 seconds. Then blend in brown sugar, and microwave about 30 seconds longer and set aside.

Drain green beans, and wrap about 8 to 9 together with a half strip bacon secured by a toothpick. Place bundles in a pyrex baking dish (9 x 13 or larger); and when all green beans are bundled, spoon the margarine mix over the top; sprinkle lightly with garlic salt, and bake at 350° for 30 to 45 minutes. Watch to see that the bacon gets cooked, but not cooked enough to shrivel up the beans.

Don't let anyone know you are fixing these, or you may not have any left to serve. You will also note that I was told that only Del Monte makes proper whole green beans for bundles.

Padre Island Shrimp Roast

5 pounds large fresh shrimp w/ heads left on (this is important, as it affects the taste of the roasted shrimp)
6 Oranges & 6 lemons — sliced very thin (remove seeds as you slice)
2 onions sliced thin
1 cup worcestershire
1 cup dry white wine
2 pounds margarine
a three ounce bottle Tabasco

Set oven on 350°; and put all in roasting pan, and cook until shrimp are done — shells turn pink & white. Serve with crusty Mexican French bread to sop up the juice and eat with the shrimp.

Summer Avocado Salad

2 avocados chopped
1 tomato chopped
1 small onion chopped
½ cup Kraft Herb & Garlic dressing

Mix together, and refrigerate at least ½ hour.

All of the animals, excepting man, know that the principal business of life is to enjoy it.

— Samuel Butler

Marinated Shrimp

4 pounds cooked peeled & deveined shrimp

Prepare marinade with a mixture of:

1 cup peanut oil
1 can beer
1/3 cup chopped fresh ginger
1 cup soy sauce
1/3 cup lime juice
1/4 cup sugar
1 cup chopped green onions
2 tablespoons lemon pepper.

Mix marinade, and bring to rolling boil for about 1 minute. Then remove from stove, and cool to room temperature. Add shrimp, and refrigerate for 3 or more hours. Then remove the shrimp from marinade, and keep shrimp in refrigerator.

Bring marinade to slow boil, and reduce heat by 50%. Remove from stove, and cool. Then add 1½ cups ketchup, and you have your dipping sauce for the shrimp (Add Tabasco if you want it hot).

HAPPY BIRTHDAY PUPPA

3 Beaten Eggs
½ Cup Grated Cheese
1 Gaines Burger

Heat skillet with a small amount of oil. Add eggs. Let cook ½ minute; then crumble gaines burger over eggs and top with cheese. Cook slowly until eggs are set and cheese melts.

Cut up on plate and let cool before you give your doggy a great birthday treat.

Potpourri Jambalaya

one 4 or 5 pound hen
2 pounds smoked sausage
2 pounds ham
1 pound yellow bell peppers
1½ pounds yellow onions
4 cloves minced garlic,
¼ cup corn oil
1 #10 can tomatoes diced
¼ cup Worcestershire sauce
1 teaspoon thyme
2 tablespoons cajun seasoning
5 cups raw rice
½ cup chopped fresh parsley
¼ cup chopped fresh cilantro.

Cook hen in large pot with about two quarts water until well done — about one hour at simmer. Heat oil in skillet; and cook garlic, onions, and peppers.

When chicken is done, remove from liquid and remove meat from bones.(Discard bones & skin). Chop chicken, ham, and sausage; add all ingredients to chicken stock and bring to boil.

Then reduce to simmer until rice is done, about 30 to 40 minutes.

This makes a lot...but it can be frozen.

Louisiana Cheese Crisps

1 cup butter or margarine
2 cups flour
8 ounces grated sharp Cheddar cheese
½ teaspoon cayenne pepper
½ teaspoon salt
2 cups Rice Krispies

Cream butter with salt and cayenne, and cut into flour. Add cheese and mix well. Then fold in Rice Krispies.

Cover mixing bowl with damp cloth and set on drainboard for 2 hours.

Knead lightly and pat teaspoon size pastry into wafers with fingers. Bake on ungreased cookie sheet about 15 minutes at 325°.

> Note: If you have one of the new air bake sheets, then you will not have to watch as closely to keep the bottoms from becoming too brown. If you don't have this type of cookie sheet, look for one in the store; for it keeps a lot of things from getting too brown on the bottom.

Also, when using the air bake pans, you will cook longer — about 20 minutes instead of 15.

These cheese crisps are so good that I just went and made some for myself.

Curry Cheese Spread

8 ounces cream cheese
8 ounces sharp cheddar grated
1 teaspoon curry powder
2 tablespoons sherry
a small jar chutney
chopped green onion tops

Mix together the cream cheese, cheddar, curry powder, and sherry; and spread into glass pie pan. Cover with chutney and sprinkle on the onion tops. I like to serve this with wheat thins.

French Silk Pie

1 9" baked pie shell
½ pound margarine or butter
1 ½ cup sugar
2 teaspoons vanilla
4 eggs
2 sq unsweetened chocolate, melted
½ pint whipping cream
1 tablespoon sugar
toasted almonds

You need a good, strong mixer for this pie. In a large mixing bowl, cream butter with sugar and vanilla. Add cold eggs, one at a time; and beat 2 minutes after adding each egg. Add the chocolate; pour into pie shell, and put in refrigerator for at least 1 hour.

Top with sweetened whipped cream . Sprinkle toasted almonds over each slice.

Baked Parmesan Cheese Noodles

8 ounce package fine egg noodles
2 cups cottage cheese
2 cups sour cream
1 cup Parmesan cheese - fresh grated
1 minced clove garlic
½ cup minced onion
¼ cup minced parsley
1 ½ teaspoon salt
dash hot pepper sauce.

Cook noodles in salted boiling water until just barely tender; then drain and rinse in cold water and set aside.

Sieve cottage cheese and beat with mixer until smooth. Combine with the remaining ingredients.

Fold sauce into noodles; put into buttered baking pyrex dish, and bake at 350° for 20-30 minutes or until the top begins to brown.

Sprinkle additional Parmesan on top when serving.

This goes well with the *Roma Meat Roll* & Italian salad.

Roma Meat Roll

1 ½ pounds ground round or extra lean beef
1 egg
¾ cup cracker crumbs (Saltines)
½ cup very finely chopped onion
two 8 ounce cans tomato sauce
1 teaspoon salt
¼ teaspoon cracked pepper
2 cups shredded Mozzarella cheese
½ teaspoon oregano

Combine beef, egg, cracker crumbs, salt, pepper, oregano, and ⅓ cup of the tomato sauce. Mix well and shape into a rectangle (about 10 x 12 on wax paper).

Spread the Mozzarella evenly over meat and roll like a jelly roll — press ends to seal. Place in shallow baking pan and cook for 1 hour at 350°.

Drain off juice; pour the remaining tomato sauce over, and cook for 15 minutes more.

For variation, use canned brown gravy instead of the tomato sauce; and add a small can of chopped mushrooms over Mozzarella before rolling up.

Summer Stuffed Tomatoes

4 large ripe tomatoes
1 pint cottage cheese
½ cup chopped cucumber
¼ cup chopped bell pepper (preferably yellow)
3 green onions chopped including tops,
½ cup mayonnaise
(mixed with 2 tablespoons Russian dressing)

Cut tops from tomatoes, and scoop out pulp into large bowl; reserve the tomato shells. Chop the tomato pulp and mix with the remaining ingredients.

Fill the tomato shells and grind some fresh black pepper on top.

The best portion of a good man's life is his little, nameless, unremembered acts of kindness and of love.
— William Wordsworth

XI

I am having so much fun writing this book, and I do hope that you are enjoying reading it. I hope that as you read this, it will fill you with memories of good food and good friends, and that the recipes here will make you want to share more time with your family and friends.

And when you share something good to eat, you know that there will be love in the room.

Sachertorte

Torte:

1 ½ sticks butter
¼ cup sugar
1 cup sifted flour
6 eggs, separated
6 ounces semisweet chocolate — melted & cooled

Apricot Filling:

1 cup apricot jam blended smooth in blender.

Glaze:

7 ounces semisweet chocolate
1 cup sugar
2/3 cup water
2 tablespoons butter

This is another recipe that requires a heavy duty mixer. Cream butter in large mixing bowl; add chocolate, and mix well. Beat in sugar, and then add egg yolks slowly with the mixer running all the time. Now remove the mixer blades. (Wash, dry, and set aside). Fold in the flour with a wooden spoon.

In a small mixing bowl, beat egg whites until they are stiff, and fold them into the batter. Pour the batter into a 9" spring form, prepared with Baker's Joy; and bake 1 hour at 350°. Cool cake about five minutes; turn out on rack, and cool completely.

When cake is completely cooled, cut in half (as if it were a bun) with a large sharp bread knife. Spread about 1/3 of the apricot in the middle, and put back together. Then spread the remaining apricot on the top and over the sides.

For the glaze, melt chocolate in top of a double boiler.

Combine the sugar and water in a sauce pan; bring to boil; reduce heat; and simmer for 5 minutes, stirring constantly.

Gradually beat sugar into chocolate; add butter, and continue to beat until the glaze is creamy.

Slowly pour hot glaze over the torte, and let some run down the sides. Then quickly spread glaze evenly with spatula; and let the torte stand for about 30 to 45 minutes, until the glaze is hard and takes on a shine.

This is a rather difficult recipe, but it is well worth it for that special dessert.

Bess's Rye Rolls

This is another recipe that takes a lot of time, so start early.

You will really enjoy having a child beside you to help on this one. In fact, this recipe brings back one of my earliest memories of cooking with Bess Maxwell. I could not have been more than 6 or 7 years old at the time.

1 package dry yeast
1 egg, beaten
¼ cup oil
1 ½ cup warm water
1 teaspoon each salt & sugar
5 cups rye flour
caraway seeds.

You will need a bottle with a very fine mist nozzle for misting these rolls just before baking. As an option, you could beat an egg white with a tablespoon of water, and brush it on with a pastry brush before sprinkling on the caraway seeds.

Here goes:

In large mixing bowl, mix water, yeast, and sugar; stir and let sit for 10 minutes. Add salt, egg, oil, and 2 cups of flour; and work to blend. Blend in the rest of the flour, a cup at a time. Mix until the dough is formed; and then cover dough in bowl, and set in warm place for an hour.

Punch down dough, and work on pastry board for about 10 minutes until the dough is smooth. Divide the dough in half, and cover with towel for 10 minutes.

Form 12 balls from each half, and place on greased baking sheet about 1 ½" apart. Slit a cross on each ball with a VERY sharp knife or a razor blade. Cover each pan with a towel, and let them rise for one hour. Remove towel; sprinkle caraway seeds on the top, and mist. Bake at 375° for 20-25 minutes.

Chicken in Plantation Sauce

Chicken:

3 pound or larger fryer (cut up)
½ teaspoon each of basil, salt, pepper, and paprika
¼ cup margarine

Mix seasonings together; and sprinkle over chicken, coating both sides. Melt the margarine in a pyrex baking dish large enough to lay the chicken in, skin side down; and bake at 400° for about 30 minutes.

Plantation Sauce:

4 tablespoons each margarine & flour
¾ cup water with two dissloved chicken bullion cubes
½ cup dry white wine.
1 can sliced mushrooms, drained
½ cup sliced green onions

While the chicken is cooking, boil water and add bullion cubes in sauce pan.

In skillet, heat margarine; add flour, and stir until it is bubbly. Turn off heat, and mix in the water and wine. Mix well to be sure there are no lumps, and you have a smooth mixture.

After the chicken has cooked for 30 minutes, remove from oven; and turn upright, and remove and discard the skin. Spread mushrooms and green onions over the chicken, and pour the sauce over all. Return to oven for another 20 minutes.

Serve over cooked rice or noodles with rye rolls (above).

Spinach in Mushroom Sauce

2 cans spinach, drained and chopped or cut with kitchen shears
1 can cream mushroom soup, undiluted
1 tablespoon butter
a dash of nutmeg.

Stir together, and heat over low heat until mixture starts to bubble. Remove immediately and serve.

This is so easy, yet so good ; and if you are looking for a way to have veggies eaten, then this should be a winner for you.

My Mama's Hot Quiche

9" pie shell
3 eggs
1 cup each grated sharp Cheddar & Mozzarella cheeses
2 cans El Chico whole chili peppers
1 tablespoon melted butter

Brush pie shell with melted butter. Remove seeds from the chilies, and spread over bottom of the pie shell.

Beat eggs, and mix in cheeses. Pour mixture over peppers. Bake at 350° for 30 minutes or until set.

Fresh Zucchini Salad

On a bed of lettuce, arrange slices of fresh zucchini; pour Russian Dressing over, and top with fresh ground pepper.

Serve with Quiche.

Russian Dressing

*One tablespoon each: Chili sauce, finely chopped
dill pickle, minced onion, and finely chopped
pimento-stuffed green olives.
½ teaspoon paprika
¼ teaspoon sugar
1 cup mayonnaise.
(3 teaspoons caviar - optional)*

Mix together, and refrigerate for about 30 minutes before serving.

This should make enough for 4 Zucchini salads.

Mississippi Cheese Grits

*1 cup grits, cooked as directed on box
¼ pound margarine
4 eggs
a large jar of Cheese Whiz (regular or jalapeno).*

Cook grits; and while still hot, put in margarine, and stir until melted. Add Cheese Whiz, and let cool at least 10 minutes.

Then add egg and beat until smooth. Put in a well greased pyrex pan (9 x 13), and place pyrex in shallow baking pan with water up about half way on the pyrex. Bake 1 hour at 350° or until set.

For variation, you can saute ¾ cup finely chopped red or green or a combination of bell peppers (use 2 tablespoons of the ¼ pound margarine to saute).

Hershey Bar Pie

6 regular size almond Hershey bars
16 marshmallows
½ cup milk
1 cup whipping cream
1 teaspoon sugar
a 9" pie shell or graham pie shell (See below)

Bake pie crust; whichever you use should be ready before you start.

Melt Hersheys in double boiler; Add marshmallows, and stir until melted.

Remove from heat; beat in milk until smooth, and let cool. Whip cream with sugar until stiff, and fold into the cooled chocolate. Pour into pie shell, and refrigerate for at least 2 hours before serving.

If you want it really fancy, then whip another cup of cream with sugar (as above), and top each slice of pie with the cream.

IMPORTANT:

I realize in writing this recipe that there are a lot of recipes that call for a pie shell, and they do take time. Soooo you can go to the super market and get unbaked pie shells in the freezer section - including a graham shell.

Graham Cracker Crust

1 ½ cup graham cracker crumbs
⅓ cup sugar
⅓ cup very soft butter.

Mix together in bowl, and press into pie pan. For baked crust, bake at 350° for about 8 to 9 minutes.

For this recipe, you can use vanilla wafers, gingersnaps, chocolate snaps or wafers, Oreo cookies; and for such things as quiche, try Rusk or Zwieback, etc.

If you don't want to try a regular pie dough, then a crumb crust is a good place to start, since it is an easy crust. There is not much that can go wrong, unless you burn it when cooking. So always check before the recommended cooking time has elapsed.

Helpful Hints

Many ovens are not set right; so you should get acquainted with your oven in order to adjust cooking times and also temperatures.

You also don't want to take something out of the oven that isn't done; so get used to testing.

Open the oven door slowly, and, close slowly.

Testing

Test custards with a table knife. Test cakes with a straw or wooden pick. In either case, the knife or straw will come out clean. If you haven't done this, ask your mother or aunt or head chef.

Too Much Salt?

Reminder about how to UN-SALT a dish: When you taste, and it's too salty - don't panic. Grate a potato into the dish. You can choose to grate on large or small grate. The small grate will make the potato less apparent, but will thicken the dish more; whereas if you use the large grate you will see more of the potato, but only slightly thicken the dish. In either case, you may have to add water or milk so that you don't get it too thick. If you are boiling beans, for example, then you can add milk and dice the potatoes and have a wonderful dish.

Hard Sugar?

If your brown sugar is hard, then put it in the microwave for 15 seconds; and if it needs a little more softening, then do 10 seconds more. Do not exceed the time I have recommended; for the sugar will turn to syrup if you get it too hot. So after the first 15 seconds, try to work it by mashing it; and then use the second 10 seconds, if needed.

Smelly Jar?

To take the smell out of a jar, try putting about ¼ cup of chlorine bleach to a gallon of water, and let it sit over night. You can also use a little comet mixed with water. The point is to fill to the brim with water and let it sit so that the bleach works out the odor.

Don't Cry!

If you find it hard to chop onions, place your cutting board next to your stove, and turn the exhaust fan on high while you cut the onions.

XII

Almond Crescents

1 cup butter or margarine
⅔ cup powdered sugar
2 cups flour
1 teaspoon almond extract
1 cup finely chopped almonds
½ cup powdered sugar to dust tops after baking

In a large mixing bowl, cream butter with sugar until light and fluffy. Add almond extract, and beat in thoroughly. Add flour, a little at a time, while beating; and and then add nuts. Knead dough into ball in bowl; cover bowl with a slightly damp towel, and refrigerate for 1 hour.

After an hour, divide the dough into 3 or 4 parts, and roll out each part to about ½ inch thick. Cut and shape the dough into crescents, as you would for Sand Tarts; and bake at 350° for about 18 minutes or until just barely brown. Cool for about 5 minutes, and dust with powdered sugar.

After dusting, let the cookies get completely cool - about 45 minutes - before you store them in covered container. These cookies are a lot like sand tarts, so you will need to hide them if you are baking them to serve at a special occasion; or they will be gone.

Strawberry Pie

Make a crumb crust from vanilla wafers, and bake it.

Filling:

½ cup butter
1 ½ cup powdered sugar
1 teaspoon vanilla
1 cup whipping cream whipped to stiff peaks
1 pint box fresh strawberries washed, dried, and sliced.

Cream together butter and sugar; fold in eggs and vanilla, and beat until light and fluffy. Fold in whipping cream. Gently fold in strawberries; reserve a few for decoration. Pour mixture into pie crust, and smooth out and decorate with reserved strawberry slices.

Refrigerate overnight, or not less than four hours.

Green Bean Casserole I

2 cans cut green beans
1 can cream of mushroom soup
1 can fried onion rings.

Drain green beans, and mix with undiluted soup. Thoroughly butter a casserole dish; then cover bottom of casserole with half of the onion rings. Pour all of the green bean and soup mixture over the onions in the baking dish. Top with remaining onion rings. Bake at 350° for about 20 minutes or until it starts to bubble.

For variation, add ½ cup grated cheese — Cheddar, Swiss, Mozzarella, etc. — to the bean and soup mixture.

Green Bean Casserole II

2 cans cut green beans
1 can cream of chicken soup
1 cup crushed potato chips.

Drain green beans, and mix with undiluted soup and ¾ cup of crushed potato chips. Pour into well buttered casserole dish and top with remaining chips. Bake at 350° for about 20 minutes, until bubbly.

Green Bean Casserole III

2 cans French cut green beans
1 can cream of mushroom soup
½ cup grated cheddar cheese
½ cup finely chopped onion
½ cup finely chopped red bell pepper
2 tablespoons margarine
1 cup crushed potato chips.

First, in a small skillet, melt margarine, and saute the onions and bell pepper in the margarine. Set aside to cool a bit, while you mix the drained green beans with the soup, cheese and ¾ cup chips. Add onion and peppers to the bean mixture; then pour into a buttered casserole dish, and top with remaining chips. Bake at 350° for 20 minutes.

For delicious variations of this recipe, or any of the green bean casseroles, use a can of corn chowder instead of cream of mushroom. The cream of mushroom is also interchangeable with cream of chicken, cream of asparagus, or most other cream soups.

Old Time Chocolate Cake

4 squares Bakers Chocolate
1 stick margarine
1 cup water

Combine the above ingredients in a pan, and heat until chocolate and margarine melt. Set aside.

In a mixing bowl, combine the following; and mix well.

2 cups flour
2 cups sugar
1 cup buttermilk
2 eggs
1 teaspoon baking soda

Add the reserved pan of chocolate liquid to the flour mixture, and mix well. Pour into a well greased bundt pan and bake 25 minutes at 350°. Test with toothpick.

Chocolate Icing

1 stick margarine
5 tablespoons milk
3 squares of Baker's Chocolate
1 pound powdered sugar
1 teaspoon vanilla

Heat the margarine, milk, and chocolate. When melted, stir until well mixed; beat in vanilla and powdered sugar; and add a little more milk if too thick. Ice this cake while it is still warm.

This is great with either Braum's or Blue Bell Homemade Vanilla Ice cream.

Cheddar Dip

10 ounce sharp Cheddar
½ can beer
¼ cup mayonnaise
1 teaspoon Worcestershire
1 teaspoon caraway seeds
½ teaspoon salt
½ teaspoon crushed red pepper

Blend together, and let sit for at least 30 minutes. Serve in small bowl with wheat thins.

Peanut Brittle

Peanut Brittle is not really hard to make if you have a candy thermometer. But this is not a rainy day project. Peanut brittle needs to be made on a dry, sunny day, or it will be sticky.

As a matter of fact, all candy is better when made on a sunny day. Even in winter, you should wait for the sun to shine before making candy.

> 2 cups sugar
> 1 cup light corn syrup
> ½ cup water
> ½ teaspoon salt
> 4 cups raw peanuts
> 2 tablespoons butter
> 2 teaspoons baking soda

Remember: A CANDY THERMOMETER IS A MUST.

In a heavy deep skillet or saucepan, heat sugar, syrup, water, and salt to a rolling boil. Add peanuts; reduce heat to medium; and cook to 293° F on candy thermometer, stirring constantly. Add butter, then baking soda, and beat very hard. Spread on buttered surface to about ¼ inch thick, and let cool. Break into pieces.

Store in airtight container.

This is not a hard recipe if you use the thermometer and work fast when spreading the brittle.

You can also make this with raw almonds.

If you want to make pecan brittle, you must watch very closely. Just as the thermometer reaches 293°, remove the brittle; and work fast to blend in butter and soda, and quickly spread; for it is easy to over cook pecans.

Reception Salad

1 package lemon Jell-o
1 large can crushed pineapple with juice,
1 pound cream cheese
1 small can pimentos
½ cup finely chopped celery
¾ cup chopped pecans
⅛ teaspoon salt
1 cup whipped cream (with 2 teaspoons sugar)

Drain pineapple juice into sauce pan; stir in Jell-o, and heat to boiling point; remove from heat and cool.

Cream the cream cheese with the chopped pimentos, celery, nuts, pineapple, and salt.

Add the Jell-o mixture, and mix well. Fold in whipped cream, and pour into mold. Refrigerate for 3 to 4 hours until well set. Unmold onto plate to serve.

Prepare your mold by "greasing " it with mayonnaise. When ready to unmold, wet a wash cloth with very hot water and wring it out; then put the cloth on the outside of the mold to slightly warm the mold.

Caviar Spread

I am really not too fond of caviar, but this spread is great.

Serve with melba toast and, as my mother noted on the bottom of this recipe, *"it makes one hell of a lot."*

Cream Cheese Mixture

Mix together:

> *1 bunch chopped green onions including tops*
> *½ cup mayonnaise*
> *1 large & 1 small package cream cheese*
> *1 tablespoon Lea & Perrin.*

Have ready:

> *7 ounces black caviar with a little lemon juice*
> *6 sieved hard cooked eggs*
> *1 bunch parsley, chopped*

Then make your spread in layers:

> *(1). Cream Cheese Mixture (above)*
> *(2). caviar with a little lemon juice*
> *(3). eggs*
> *(4). chopped parsley*

Keep in refrigerator until serving time.

Strawberry Ice Box Pie
or
Chocolate Ice Box Pie

Prepare a 9" graham crust, and bake.

Cream together ½ cup powdered sugar and 8 ounces cream cheese, and spread as bottom layer in pie crust.

Strawberry Pie:
1 ½ pint strawberries, mashed
(the other ½ pint sliced and reserved to garnish top of pie)
1 cup sugar
3 tablespoons corn starch

Cook strawberries over low heat with sugar and corn starch until thickened, about 10 minutes. *Cool before pouring over cream cheese layer.*

Top with 1 cup whipping cream, whipped with 1 tablespoon sugar, and strawberry slices.

Chocolate Pie:
2 large packages Instant Chocolate Pudding Mix
3 cups milk
½ bowl Cool Whip (the other half is for topping).

Beat together the pudding, milk, and Cool Whip until it starts to thicken. Spread over cream cheese, and top with the remaining Cool Whip. For variation: add ½ teaspoon Meyers Dark Rum to pudding.

... Pies should be prepared 2 hours ahead & refrigerated.

Texas Tortilla Casserole

For this to be a success, you must use *FRESH* grated Parmesan cheese.

1 pound ground beef
1 can whole kernel corn
15 ounce can tomato sauce
1 cup picante - mild, medium, or hot as you like
1 tablespoon chili powder
1 ½ teaspoon cumin.

1 pound cottage cheese
2 eggs
½ cup fresh grated parmesan cheese
1 teaspoon oregano
½ teaspoon garlic salt

12 corn tortillas cut in strips about 2" wide

1 cup each grated Cheddar & Monterrey Jack cheeses, mixed together

Brown and crumble the beef, and drain off the grease. Then drain the corn; and add to meat, along with the tomato sauce, picante, chili powder, and cumin. Cook at simmer for about 5 minutes.

In medium bowl, beat together the cottage cheese, eggs, parmesan, oregano, and garlic salt.

Spread ½ the meat mixture into a 9 x 13 pyrex pan, and cover with half the tortilla strips. Next layer the cottage cheese mix over the tortilla strips.

Put another layer of tortilla strips on top of the cottage cheese mix; then cover with remaining meat mixture.

Top with the Cheddar and Jack cheese, and bake at 350° for about 30 minutes or until bubbly.

Coconut Raisin Oatmeal Cookies

1 cup flour
½ cup sugar
½ cup brown sugar
⅓ cup margarine
1 egg
1 teaspoon vanilla
½ teaspoon each baking soda & baking powder
½ cup coconut
⅔ cup plumped raisins
½ cup oatmeal.

Cream together margarine and sugars; add egg and vanilla. Beat well.

Add all other ingredients, and mix thoroughly to form dough.

Shape into balls about the size of walnuts, and bake on an ungreased cookie sheet at 375° for 12 to 15 minutes.

Butterscotch Bars

4 eggs
1 pound brown sugar
2 cups Bisquick mix
2 cups chopped walnuts or pecans
6 ounce package butterscotch morsels
1 teaspoon vanilla

Beat eggs with mixer until frothy. Gradually add sugar, beating until thick; then add the remaining ingredients.

Pour into a 9 x 13 pyrex baking pan, previously sprayed with Baker's Joy. Bake for 55 minutes at 325°.

Let cool and cut into bars.

XIII

Key Lime Pie

A 9" pie shell (half - baked)
4 eggs, separated (three egg whites in one bowl and one egg white in another bowl)
1 can Eagle Brand Condensed Milk
½ cup lime juice
1 tablespoon finely grated lime rind
½ teaspoon cream of tartar
⅓ cup sugar.

Beat egg yolks with milk, lime juice, and grated rind.

In a small bowl, beat the one egg white until stiff and fold into lime mix. (You can use green food coloring if you want this to look green). Pour lime mix into cooled pie shell.

Beat the three egg whites until frothy; then sprinkle cream of tartar and sugar in, and beat until it forms peaks. Spread meringue over filling, making sure that meringue touches the edge of the pie shell so that it will not "shrink" as it is cooking. Bake at 350° for about 15 minutes.

Be sure to refrigerate the pie if you don't plan to serve it within a few hours of making it.

German Chocolate Pie

1 unbaked 9" pie shell
4 ounces semisweet chocolate
¼ cup margarine
13 ounce can evaporated milk
3 eggs slightly beaten
1 cup chopped pecans
1 ⅓ cup coconut

Melt chocolate and butter over low heat. Remove from heat. Add milk, eggs, sugar, and coconut; and mix well. Stir in pecans, and pour into pie shell. Bake at 375° for 30 minutes. This pie also needs to be kept in the refrigerator.

Eagle Brand Brownies

Melt together:

12 ounce package chocolate chips
½ stick butter
1 can Eagle Brand.

Do not Boil...Remove from heat and stir in:

1 cup flour
1 teaspoon vanilla
1 cup pecans

Mix well.

Spray cookie sheet with Pam; pour mixture on; spread it out, and bake at 350° for about 8 to 10 minutes. Cool and cut.

Serves well with vanilla ice cream over a square.

Smoked Turkey Ball

1 cup fine chopped smoked turkey
8 ounces cream cheese
½ cup chopped pecans
2 tablespoons mayonnaise
Chopped parsley.

Mix turkey, cream cheese, pecans, and mayonnaise. When well blended, roll into a ball and coat with chopped parsley.

Serve with water crackers.

Asparagus Salad

1 can cream of asparagus soup
8 ounces cream cheese
1 tablespoon dehydrated onion
1 tablespoon lemon juice
¾ cup mayonnaise
1 cup chopped celery
1 cup chopped pecans
1 package Knox gelatin dissolved in ½ cup warm water
1 can asparagus spears.

Heat soup - undiluted. Add cream cheese; mix well and remove from heat. Beat in mayonnaise, lemon juice, and then gelatin. Mix very well; and fold in celery, nuts, and onion.

Grease an 8" square pyrex pan with mayonnaise, and pour mixture in. Top with the asparagus spears. Chill for at least 1 ½ hours, and serve.

Tennessee Corn Casserole

2 - 16 ounce cans cream style corn
1 cup Bisquick
1 egg, beaten,
2 tablespoons olive oil
½ cup milk
1 - 5 ounce can chopped chili pepers (El Chico)

Combine and mix well all ingredients, except chili peppers; and put ½ of the mixture in 8 x 8 "Pamed" pyrex dish.

Add a layer of chopped chili peppers, and cover with remaining corn mixture.

Top with 1 ½ cups grated Monterrey Jack cheese, and bake at 350° for about 25 to 30 minutes.

Great soul food — the kind that inspires oohs and ahs from your family or guests —is in direct proportion to how much you enjoyed cooking it. As Ralph Waldo Emerson once said:

> *"Nothing great was ever achieved without enthusiasm."*.

Oatmeal Banana Nut Bread

½ cup Crisco
1 cup sugar
2 eggs
1 cup mashed banana
½ cup Oatmeal
1 teaspoon soda
1 teaspoon vanilla
¾ cup chopped pecans
1 ½ cup flour
¼ teaspoon salt

Sift together flour, soda, and salt. Cream together sugar and crisco. Add eggs, one at a time. Add banana and vanilla, and beat well. Add flour and oats into cream mixture, and mix well. Then fold in nuts. Spray Baker's Joy in a 9 x 5 loaf pan, and pour in batter.

Bake at 350° for 50 to 60 minutes. Test with straw. Cool 5 minutes before turning out of pan. Let bread cool completely on wire rack for at least an hour. Then wrap in foil and refrigerate.

Sweet Potato Casserole

3 cups mashed cooked sweet potatoes (fresh or canned)
2 eggs
1 stick butter
½ cup white sugar
1 teaspoon vanilla
⅓ cup milk

Mix all ingredients together, and pour in casserole dish.

Top with a mixture of:

> *⅓ cup butter*
> *1 cup light brown sugar*
> *½ cup flour*
> *1 cup chopped pecans.*

Bake at 350° for about 25 to 30 minutes.

Noel's Swiss Cheese Ball

> *1 pound grated Baby Swiss cheese*
> *1 bunch green onions, very finely chopped (Save the green tops)*
> *Mayonnaise*

Mix ingredients together and form into a ball, using enough mayonnaise to make it bind. Roll ball in onion tops.

Turnip Greens with Cornmeal Dumplings

Turnip Greens:

> *About 2 pounds meaty ham hocks*
> *3 to 4 pounds turnip greens with roots*
> *2 quarts water*
> *Dash of pepper*

Wash ham hocks in cold water, and place in large pot on stove with 2 quarts water. Boil for about an hour.

Wash and clean turnips, removing pulpy stems and any spots on leaves. Peel roots, and cut in halves or quarters. Cut leaves, and put roots and leaves in with the ham hock. Add a dash of pepper, and cover and simmer for about an hour longer.

Dumplings:

1 cup cornmeal
1 teaspoon sugar
½ teaspoon salt
½ cup flour
1 ½ cup boiling water
1 egg beaten

Combine cornmeal, sugar, and salt; and stir in boiling water. Add egg and mix well. Turn out onto board with the flour on it; roll the dough in flour, and shape into dumplings.

Remove cover from the turnip pot, and place the dumplings on top of greens. Put cover back on, and let the pot simmer for about 10 to 20 minutes. Turn off heat, and keep covered until you are ready to serve.

Cashew Nut Butter

Grind in food processor:

one 10 ounce can cashews
½ teaspoon olive oil

Process until smooth, adjusting oil as necessary.

This will make about a cup of butter. It keeps at room temperature for about 10 days.

The flavor is much better if you make small batches, rather than double this recipe and refrigerate the butter. This is wonderful on a toasted bun for breakfast, and even better on vanilla wafers for a snack.

When buying nuts for this, you can use bits, halves, or pieces. You don't need to buy whole or fancy or any extra large nuts.

Virgina Honey Nut Butter

Grind in food processor:

1 - 10 ounce can honey roast or toffee nuts
olive oil

As above, the amount of oil will depend on the nuts; but add a little at a time, and grind at least one minute after adding oil before you add more.

You will probably have to remove the top of your food processor and scrape the sides when you are grinding nuts into butter.

Richard's Pasta Salad

12 ounce package veggie shells
(the multi colored kind)

Cook according to package directions, BUT WITHOUT SALT. Drain and wash in cold water, and leave in colander while you mix dressing.

Pasta Salad Dressing

1 cup mayonnaise
½ cup sour cream
½ cup chopped fresh cilantro
1 teaspoon garlic salt
1 each yellow, green, red bell peppers,
seeded and chopped
2 zucchini squash
(cut in strips, like dill strips, and then sliced thinly)
1 bunch green onions, sliced thin
1 cup fresh grated Parmesan cheese.

Mix the mayonnaise, sour cream, cilantro, and garlic salt; and blend well. In a large bowl, pour in the cooled pasta shells and the chopped veggies. Pour the mayonnaise dressing over, and toss to coat everything. Refrigerate covered for at least 30 minutes.

You could make this in the morning, and serve at night or the next day. Just before serving, top with the parmesan cheese and gently toss.

For variation, you can add a small can of green peas to this salad and/or a cup of either Cheddar or Swiss cheese, cut into very small cubes. You can also use yellow squash in place of or along with the zucchini squash.

If you use the 16 ounce package of pasta shells, increase the dressing to 1½ cups mayonnaise, 1 cup sour cream, and 2 teaspoons garlic salt. Leave everything else the same.

Cheese Rice Casserole

3 cups cooked rice
1 cup sour cream
1 teaspoon salt
¼ teaspoon cayenne pepper
¾ cup each grated Cheddar and Monterrey Jack cheeses

Grate the cheeses into a bowl; and toss together to mix. Remove ½ of the cheese to use for topping. Combine the other half of the cheese with the rice, sour cream, salt, and pepper. Pour into a buttered casserole dish, and top with the remaining cheese.

Bake at 350° for 20 minutes.

True Lasagna

1 pound ground beef
1 onion, chopped
1 red bell pepper, chopped
2 - 8 ounce cans tomato sauce
½ teaspoon each garlic salt, fresh ground pepper,
crushed fennel seed
1 teaspoon Italian seasoning
1 tablespoon dry parsley flakes
1 - 8 ounce package lasagna noodles
1 pint small curd cottage cheese
1 cup sour cream
1 - 3 ounce package cream cheese
1 pound grated Mozzarella cheese
1 cup fresh grated Parmesan cheese.

Cook the lasagna noodles without salt, as the package directs. Drain and rinse in colander.

In medium bowl, grate the cheeses, and toss to mix together.

In another bowl, cream together the sour cream and cream cheese. Add the cottage cheese, and set aside.

In large skillet, cook meat, onion, and bell pepper until meat is browned and you can crumble it up. Spoon off as much of the drippings as you can; and add the tomato sauce, garlic salt, fennel, black pepper, Italian seasoning, and parsley.

Stir well and simmer for about 25 minutes to tighten the meat sauce. Stir to make sure you aren't cooking too fast.

To assemble the lasagna, layer in a 9 x 13 pyrex baking dish that you have sprayed with Pam.

You will use half of each of the above, so you have two layers of each in the following order:

first a layer of noodles
next a layer of the cottage cheese mix
next meat sauce
and last the grated cheese.

Repeat second layer in the same order, and bake at 350° for 30 to 40 minutes.

Remove from oven and let it stand for 10 to 15 minutes before serving.

To serve, take a sharp knife and cut into serving size squares, (as if you were cutting brownies) so that when you lift out with spatula, the noodles are cut and everything doesn't fall apart.

While you are letting this set up, you can toast some garlic bread, and fix a good tossed salad or sliced tomatoes for a complete meal.

Cranapple Muffins

¾ cup diced unpeeled tart apple
¾ cup frozen cranberries
1 egg
¾ cup packed dark brown sugar
¼ cup butter
1 teaspoon vanilla
1 cup flour
½ cup oatmeal
1 teaspoon baking powder
¼ teaspoon salt
1 teaspoon cinnamon

Note: If you use fresh cranberries, you need to bring about 1 quart of water to a boil, dump in the cranberries, and immediately put pan under cold running water, and drain.

In a large bowl, mix flour, oats, baking powder, salt, and cinnamon.

In small bowl, mix butter, sugar, and vanilla. Beat until smooth, and then beat in egg. Add apple and cranberries; pour this over the flour mixture, and blend just until dough forms.

Spray muffin pan with Baker's Joy, and fill with dough to about ¾ full. This recipe should make 12 regular size muffins. Spoon a little dough into each muffin cup: and then finish by trying to fill each cup equally, so that all muffins will bake at the same speed.

Bake at 350° for 20 to 25 minutes. Cool about 5 minutes in pan; and then turn onto rack, and cool completely (about 1 ½ hour).

Wrap individual muffins with plastic wrap for school lunches. Store unwrapped muffins in airtight container.

Ham & Cheese Rollups

*1 cup grated cheese (Cheddar, Swiss,
Monterrey Jack, or any combination
- even flavored such as jalapeno or caraway seed)
2 tablespoons mayonnaise
3 tablespoons chopped olive (spanish or black)
8 thin slices of ham from deli.*

Make a mixture of the cheese, mayonnaise, and olive. Spread on ham slices, and roll like a jelly roll; secure with four toothpicks so that you can slice each ham slice into quarters, i.e. 32 pieces.

With the above, you can make several variations for an easy party tray.

Cover with plastic wrap, and refrigerate if not serving right away.

XIV

Melba's Garlic Sweet Pickles

1 gallon large whole sour pickles
3 pounds white sugar
16 cloves garlic
2 boxes (1 ½ ounce each) pickling spices
about a quart good cider vinegar

You will need a two gallon crock pot with cover for making these.

Drain and wash pickles, and cut into thick slices. Peel and chip garlic.

Alternate layers of pickles, spices, sugar, and garlic, putting sugar on top. Then pour in vinegar to cover.

Stir each day for 7 to 10 days. Pickles will be ready in 7 days in summer, but it takes 10 days in winter.

Seal in jars, and store in cool place. Refrigerate after opening jar.

Richard's Garlic Dill Pickles

1 gallon large whole dill pickles
5 pounds white sugar
16 cloves garlic
1 box pickling spices
1 tablespoon whole cloves
about a pound of fresh seranno peppers
about a quart of good white vinegar.

Drain and rinse the pickles, and cut into thick slices. Peel and chip the garlic.

Alternate layers of pickles, spices, garlic and sugar, using sugar as top layer. Pour vinegar to cover.

Stir each day at least twice for 7 to 10 days — seven in summer, ten in the winter. Seal the pickles in jars, and give at least half to friends. Store in cool place. Refrigerate after opening jar.

As the pickles are eaten, I often put leftover sliced onions in the juice and after a few days in the refrigerator, they also acquire a great flavor.

Also, as far as peppers go, I have used banana peppers and cortina peppers, but I don't recommend jalapeno peppers, because their flavor does not blend with the pickles — at least to suit my taste.

If you don't have a crock pot, you can make these pickles by using the gallon jar that the pickles come in; but it is harder to stir the pickles. I always use a wooden spoon and gently stir, so as not to break up the pickles.

You NEVER want to use any type of metal when making pickles. You can also use a large bowl to make the pickles (as long as you can cover it).

Corn Relish

When you make Sweet Garlic Pickles, you will have some juice left over; and since it is not inexpensive to make the pickles, I don't throw the extra juice away. It makes wonderful relish.

This recipe will depend on how much juice you have left over; I usually make it with three of each of the following:

> *1 can whole kernel corn per cup of juice*
> *1 red bell pepper per cup of juice*
> *1 med white onion per cup of juice*
> *1/2 teaspoon cornstarch per cup of juice*

Open can or cans; pour corn into colander, and wash in cold water. Let it drain while you chop the red pepper and onion. Then toss the corn, peppers, and onion in the colander.

Strain the leftover juice into a large stainless steel or glass sauce pan, and add ½ teaspoon corn starch for each cup of juice. Stir well, bring to boiling point. Then remove from heat.

Stir corn mixture into hot juice. Then fill jars, leaving about ½ inch of space at top. Let the jars cool for 15 minutes; then seal with lids.

Note: before you fill jars, run hot tap water into jars to warm them.

Jalapeno Cornbread

3 cups yellow cornbread mix
3 eggs
2 1/4 cups milk
1/2 cup oil or bacon drippings
1 tablespoon sugar
1 large onion grated
1 can cream style corn
1 1/2 cup grated medium cheddar cheese
5 to 10 chopped pickled jalapeno peppers, according to taste (if using mild peppers, you may want to double the amount of peppers).

Mix all together, and bake in hot greased pan at 425° for 10 to 12 minutes.

To prepare baking pan, heat it in the oven until pan is very hot. Then spoon grease into pan; if you are using bacon drippings, it will usually sizzle.

Spoon batter into the pan while still hot, and immediately return to oven.

I recommend cast iron pans — corn stick or the divided skillet which makes wedges — for the very best cornbread.

Krazy Apple Krisp

6 cups chopped zucchini
3 cups chopped Granny Smith apples
6 tablespoons lemon juice
3 tablespoons quick cooking tapioca
¾ cup sugar
½ teaspoon cinnamon

1 ⅓ cup flour
½ cup oatmeal flakes
⅔ cup firmly packed dark brown sugar
¼ teaspoon coriander
¼ teaspoon nutmeg
½ cup margarine

Mix together the zucchini, apples, lemon juice, tapioca, white sugar, and cinnamon. Set aside.

Mix the flour, oats, brown sugar, coriander & nutmeg. Cut in the margarine to make it a crumbly mix for the topping.

Butter a large (3 or 4 quart) covered casserole dish, and spread the zucchini and apple mix on bottom. Spread the flour mix over the top, and cover and bake at 350° for 20 minutes.

Remove cover, and continue baking for 10 to 15 minutes longer to "Krisp" the topping.

Let this cool to just warm before serving.

Half & Half Topping

In the morning, for use that evening, open a pint of half & half and add 2 to 3 tablespoons sugar in the spout. Close spout; shake well and put in refrigerator; and 3 to 4 times during the day when you open the refrigerator, shake the carton. This sweet cream will be ready to pour over your Krazy Apple Krisp at dinner.

Spanish Green Beans

6 strips bacon
½ cup chopped onion
2 tablespoons finely chopped red bell pepper
1 ½ tablespoons flour
2 cans French cut green beans
1 16 ounce can stewed tomatoes
Salt
Fresh ground pepper

Fry bacon until crisp. Remove to paper towel, and add onion and bell pepper to drippings. Cook until tender; then stir in flour. Cut up the tomatoes; crumble the bacon, and add all ingredients to the pan. Salt and pepper to taste.

Turn this mixture into a buttered 2 or 3 quart casserole, and bake at 350° for 30 minutes.

A truly elegant taste is generally accompanied with excellency of heart.
—Henry Fielding.

Cream Cheese Pie

CRUST:

1 ½ cup crushed vanilla wafers
¼ pound margarine
3 tablespoons sugar

Let margarine come to room temperature, and then mix well with sugar. Mix in the vanilla wafer crumbs, and press into a 9 inch pie pan. Do not cook.

FILLING:

12 ounces cream cheese
½ cup sugar
2 eggs
1 teaspoon vanilla
¼ teaspoon cinnamon

Bring the cream cheese to room temperature, and beat in sugar. Add the eggs, one at a time, and then the vanilla. Mix well.

Pour filling into crust, and bake at 350° for 20 minutes. Remove from oven, and let it stand for about 30 minutes before you put on topping.

TOPPING:

1 cup sour cream
2 tablespoons sugar
½ teaspoon vanilla

Combine all ingredients, and spread over filling. Bake 5 minutes at 450°.

East Texas Brownies

2 squares unsweetened chocolate
½ cup flour, sifted
¼ cup margarine
1 cup sugar
2 eggs beaten
¼ teaspoon salt
1 teaspoon vanilla
1 cup chopped pecans.

In top of double boiler, melt chocolate and margarine. Remove from heat and cool 5 minutes. Then add eggs and sugar, and beat well. Add the flour, salt, vanilla, and ½ cup pecans; and mix into batter. Pour batter into an 8" square pyrex pan, prepared with Baker's Joy, and sprinkle remaining nuts over top, pressing them into batter with your fingers. Bake at 300°, yes that is 300°, for about 45 minutes. These are chewy, and they are really good topped with vanilla ice cream.

Cool uncovered in the refrigerator.

Alabama Mushroom Chicken

4 boneless chicken breasts, pounded
½ pound fresh mushrooms, sliced
1 small onion, chopped
3 tablespoons margarine
½ cup olive oil
1 ½ cup grated Mozzarella cheese
salt and pepper
flour

Saute mushrooms and onion in margarine in a small skillet.

In large iron skillet, heat oil; coat chicken with salt, pepper and flour, and fry till done (about 10 minutes). Then remove skillet from stove, and spoon mushrooms and onions over the chicken and top with the grated cheese. Place under broiler in oven to melt cheese. This won't take long; so watch it so you can remove when the cheese just starts to turn golden.

Chocolate Nut Butter

This is something like Nutella. It is a chocolate spread, which is fan-tas-tic at breakfast. Spread on a croissant, that has been split and buttered lightly and then toasted in a skillet. Also, it is so easy to make.

1 large chocolate bar with hazelnuts
(or almonds, or peanuts)
two or three tablespoons salted real butter.

Break the chocolate bar up; put in food processor, and add butter, 1 tablespoon at a time, until the mixture is a spread. The amount of butter depends on how large the chocolate bar is and how "wet" you like the spread.

> Note: The chocolate bar must be at room temperature; also this spread requires less butter when made in the summer. Keep spread at room temperature in a cool place for a week; otherwise you will need to refrigerate this and bring to room temperature each time you serve it. So make in batches small enough to eat in a week.

This is also a great after school snack on grahams or vanilla wafers.

Chili Rice

4 cups cooked rice
3 cups sour cream
¾ cup chopped canned green chilies
½ teaspoon salt
¼ teaspoon cayenne pepper
¾ pound grated Monterrey Jack cheese
½ cup grated mild Cheddar cheese

Mix sour cream, rice, chilies, salt and pepper. Pour ½ rice mixture into buttered 2 quart casserole; cover with ½ the grated Monterrey Jack. Layer remaining rice mixture, then Monterrey Jack and top off with the Cheddar.

Bake at 350° for 25 minutes.

Georgia Sweet Potato Biscuits

1 cup mashed sweet potatoes
2 ½ cups Bisquick
½ cup margarine
½ cup milk
2 tablespoons white sugar

Mix all ingredients to form dough ball. Knead 3 times, and roll out to ½ inch thick on floured board.

Use biscuit cutter to cut, and place on ungreased baking sheet with edges touching. Bake at 400° for 10 to 12 minutes.

XV

Broccoli Rice Casserole

5 fresh mushrooms chopped
½ cup chopped celery
½ cup chopped onion
2 tablespoons olive oil
1 ten ounce package frozen chopped broccoli
1 can cream of broccoli soup
½ cup sour cream
1 cup grated Velveeta cheese
2 cups cooked brown rice

Saute mushroom, onion, and celery in oil.

In a large bowl, combine the soup and sour cream; then add sauted veggies, broccoli, cheese, and rice.

Pour into 2 quart casserole dish, which has been sprayed with Pam.

Bake 30 minutes at 350°.

. . . Even George Bush could like this. . . .

Texas Trash

To make this you will need:

two large roasting pans
or
two large 12 x 16 baking pans about 4" deep

1 package each:

Cheerios
Wheat Chex
Rice Chex
Corn Chex
pretzel sticks
pretzel O's

and

2 lbs. nuts - peanuts, cashews, mixed nuts,
or whatever you desire.

You can omit the nuts or even double the nuts to suit your taste.

Sauce:

1 pound margarine
1 ½ cup Worcestershire
1 cup Louisiana Hot Sauce (Not Tabasco)
1 tablespoon Liquid Smoke

Heat margarine and liquids together; when hot, stir in nuts to coat well. Then spoon nuts and liquid over over the mixed cereals. Toss gently to coat well.

Spread coated cereal into baking pans. Put in low oven at 200°, and let dry out slowly for 4 to 6 hours.

You will need to remove from the oven about every hour or so and gently toss to prevent the cereal from sticking together. In order for it to become thoroughly dry, you may have to cook it longer.

Cool at least two hours before putting into airtight containers.

You can get decorated tins at the drug or grocery store to fill for gifts, or make your own by spray painting coffee cans.

This recipe makes a lot, but after you give some away and everyone at home starts getting into it, you will think it really didn't make that much.

Crustless Quiche

3 eggs
1 cup sharp Cheddar
1 cup Mozzarella
2 cans El Chico whole chili peppers

Split peppers and remove seeds. Butter 9 x 13 pyrex and spread peppers over bottom.

Mix eggs and cheese and pour over peppers. Bake at 350° for 30 minutes.

As a variation, you can add 1 cup chopped boiled ham to the eggs and cheese.

Cheese Soup

2 tablespoons margarine
1 cup finely chopped celery
1 cup finely chopped onion
6 chicken bullion cubes
3 cups water
½ teaspoon fresh ground pepper
1 box frozen broccoli cauliflower and carrots
(cut in small chunks)
1 cup shredded potatoes
1 quart whole milk
2 ½ cups grated mild or medium Cheddar cheese.

In dutch oven, cook onions and celery in margarine until tender. Then add water, bullion cubes, pepper, potatoes, and vegetables; and boil uncovered for 30 minutes until very tender.

Add milk and cheese, and stir over low heat until cheese is melted. Do not let the soup boil after adding milk and cheese.

If you want a really thick soup, use half & half instead of milk.

Remoulade Sauce

2 cups mayonnaise
½ cup creole mustard
2 tablespoons salad mustard
1 tablespoon horseradish
1 tablespoons Worcestershire sauce
2 tablespoons chopped capers
½ cup finely chopped white onion
a dash of Tabasco

Mix all ingredients together, and put in covered jar in refrigerator for at least an hour before serving.

Chopped Liver

Rinse and broil 1 pound calf liver, turning at least once, until done; then chop and remove any strings.

Chop 2 large white onions, and saute in chicken fat.

Chop 6 hard-boiled eggs.

Mix all ingredients together, and season with garlic salt and course ground pepper. Add more chicken fat if necessary to bind.

This can also be made with chicken livers if desired.

Dumplings

Sift together 2 cups flour, 4 teaspoons baking powder, and 1/2 teaspoon salt. Gradually add 1 cup of milk, stirring as you pour in the milk.

To cook, drop by spoonfuls on top of cooked meat about 15 to 20 minutes before it is ready to serve. ***Cover tightly,*** and steam for 15 minutes or so.

The secret of good dumplings is to ***keep the lid tightly closed for at least 15 minutes,*** so the dumplings will be light. If you let the steam escape, then your dumplings are going to be heavy and soggy and tough; so do not lift the lid while cooking.

If you have baked a chicken, then pour the broth into a deep skillet on the top of the stove, and make your dumplings in it with the lid on.

A RECIPE FOR LIFE

GOD, grant me the serenity to accept the things I cannot change, the strength to change the things I can, AND, the wisdom to know the difference"

Amen. So mote it be.

I do not know where this originated, but it is a great comfort when you need to reflect on your problems and solutions each day of your life.

For best results, ***repeat it often.***

XVI

Baked Ham Hash

2 pounds cooked ham, trimmed and finely chopped
4 medium potatoes, boiled and cut in small cubes
1 onion, chopped
½ cup chopped parsley
½ tsp. salt
½ teaspoon fresh ground pepper
¼ teaspoon sage
⅛ teaspoon nutmeg
½ cup whipping cream
8 eggs
about ½ a stick of butter sliced into eight pats.

Preheat oven to 375°. Spray a 9x13 pyrex with Pam.

Mix together all items, except eggs and butter. Press into pyrex dish, and smooth out with fingers. Then with a spoon, make eight depressions, and put a pat of butter in each depression. Bake for 20 minutes; carefully remove from oven — don't slosh butter — and put an egg in each depression. Return to oven and cook about 5 or 6 minutes longer, or until eggs are cooked. Cut into squares and use spatula to serve.

Baking Powder Biscuits

2 ½ cups flour
1 ½ Tablespoon baking powder
5 Tablespoons Crisco shortening
- at room temperature
½ teaspoon salt
1 cup milk (use whole milk)

Preheat oven to 450°.

Sift together flour, salt, and baking powder into a large bowl, and work shortening into flour until you have a consistency similar to oatmeal flakes. Do this as quickly as possible, and try not to over work.

Now add milk, and again work as little as possible to form dough. Place dough onto floured board; knead lightly, and roll out to ½ to ¾ inch thick. Cut with biscuit cutter or glass, and place biscuits on baking sheet that has been prepared with Baker's Joy. Bake about 10 to 12 minutes or until just brown on top.

Note: I prefer my biscuits light and high; so I try to keep my dough ¾ inch thick.

Buttermilk Biscuits

To the above recipe, add ½ teaspoon baking soda to dry ingredients; and use buttermilk instead of whole milk. Otherwise, it is the same.

There are two secrets to good biscuits: one is not to over work the dough, and the other is to have the oven good and hot when you put the biscuits in. Try to look through the door glass and not open the oven until the biscuits are done; for any cooling of the oven during cooking will make your biscuits come out heavy.

Bean and Sausage Stew

1 ½ pound Great Northern Beans
1 pound sliced bacon, cut crosswise into ½ inch pieces
2 pounds trimmed lamb, cut into small cubes
1 pound Chorizo Sausage
4 onions, chopped
3 cloves garlic, minced
1 small can tomato paste (4 ounce)
⅛ teaspoon thyme
⅛ teaspoon rosemary
2 tablespoons chopped parsley
1 teaspoon salt
1 teaspoon fresh ground pepper
6 cups water
6 beef bullion cubes

Soak beans over night; and then wash and cover with salted water, and cook about 2 hours, until just tender (but maybe not fully done).

Put bacon in large dutch oven on top of stove, and cook bacon until it starts to brown. Add lamb, and brown meat; add onions and garlic, and cook on low heat until the onions are clear.

Add the remaining ingredients, except sausage and beans, and bake in 350° oven for one hour.

Stir in beans and sausage, which has been cut into ¼ inch rounds, and bake another 30 to 40 minutes.

Serve with *fried green tomatoes* and cornbread.

Fried Green Tomatoes

*6 to 7 green tomatoes
(or whatever you need for the meal)
2 eggs beaten with ½ cup milk
a cup or more of cornmeal mixed with
2 tablespoons flour*

Fried tomatoes are best cooked just before mealtime. Pare and slice tomatoes about ¼ inch thick, and chill in refrigerator at least one hour.

Before you take the tomatoes out of the refrigerator, heat about ½ inch of oil in a heavy skillet.

Dip the tomato slices into the egg-milk mixture; coat with cornmeal, and fry about one minute on each side.

Drain on paper towels, and serve while still warm and crisp.

If you don't have green tomatoes, then you can use this recipe for frying sliced white squash, or other veggies. Here again, the trick is to prepare the veggies and chill; and then cook them right before serving.

XVII

TEXAS TAMALES

Tamales are really not hard to make, but they do take a lot of time and preparation.

The following will make about two dozen tamales.

(Read the masa dough part now, because you need to get a pound of margarine out to let it get really soft.)

Filling:

> 2 pounds ground hot sausage
> One Package Lawry's Taco Seasoning Mix
> ½ cup hot water

Cook sausage to crumble stage, and drain grease. Add the seasoning mix and water, and slowly simmer for about ½ hour.

Shucks:

While the meat is cooking, carefully remove the shucks from 8 to 10 ears of corn. Clean silks from the shucks. Wash shucks and cover with a wet (very wet) towel to keep them moist and pliable.

You can use cotton string to tie your tamales, but I use strips of the shucks - use what ever you find works best for you.

The Masa Dough:

3 cups masa harina
1 pound margarine
1 ½ cup milk
2 teaspoons baking powder
1 teaspoon garlic salt

Whip the soft margarine together with baking powder and garlic salt. Next add the masa harina, and mix well together; this can be done best with a heavy duty electric mixer.

To this, add about a cup of milk to form the masa dough. Gradually add more milk to get the dough to a working consistency. You will need to be able to pat the dough out so that you can fill it with the meat mix and then roll the shuck around the tamale.

Note: Instead of milk, I use a 10 ounce can of Franco American Turkey Gravy mixed with milk to make 1 ½ cup. This gives the masa dough a great flavor.

Cooking:

Steam tamales either in a pressure cooker for about 10 minutes or over a hot water steam in a large kettle for about an hour. Let the tamales cool for about 15 minutes before serving.

Wrap any leftover tamales in foil, and store in refrigerator. If you want to freeze, wrap in plastic wrap and then in foil to keep airtight in freezer.

To reheat, put about ¼ inch water in a sauce pan and a single layer of tamales. Heat covered over low heat for about 20 minutes. Do not try to heat too fast, as it will make the masa tough.

Tamale Pie

If you get tired of making tamales, then you can make a pie by pressing the masa dough into a pie pan, casserole dish, or whatever.

Press the dough up the sides of the container and keep it fairly thin. Fill with meat. Then pat out the top crust and cover mixture.

Smooth the top, and join the edges of the top and side crusts.

Bake at 350° until the top starts to turn light yellow. Top with grated cheese, while hot.

This should cook in about 20 minutes, but it depends on how large a pie you've made. Watch it, so as not to over cook.

Pico-de-Gallo

Wash, trim, and then chop one bunch of cilantro in you food processor.

Put this on bottom of a 2 quart glass jar.

Next chop four large fresh jalapeno peppers in processor and put into jar.

Now chop a large Spanish or 10/15 onion (this should be a 1 pound or more onion) and put in jar.

Next cut the stem part from 10 small salad tomatoes; quarter them, and chop in processor - only two or three at a time — and put into jar. (10 small salad tomatoes should be about 2 pounds of tomatoes).

Add one tablespoon garlic salt on top of the tomatoes in the jar, and squeeze the juice of a large lime over the salt.

Put the lid on the jar, and refrigerate for at least four hours. Pour this out into a large bowl; mix well, and it is ready to serve. Keep what you are not serving in the refrigerator.

Because this is a fresh salad mixture (without additives or preservatives), it will keep only a few days. If you want to keep it longer, you will have to pour into sauce pan, cook it, and use it as salsa.

XVIII

A copyright is something that I don't understand as far as cook books go. Even though this is a copyrighted collection, I really want you to use all these recipes and change them as you like (which makes them your recipes).

In fact, I really don't care if you copy them word for word and claim that they are your own.....BECAUSE I did not create very many of these from "just out of my head." I learned from others, and this is what I want to share with you. So I give to you all the recipes in this book, and I do NOT reserve anything; for this is a labor of love, which I sincerely hope brings joy and happiness to you and your home.

Parmesan - Cream Cheese Spread

4 ounce cream cheese
1 teaspoon Italian Herbs
2 tablespoons fresh grated parmesan cheese

Mix together with fork, and let it set for awhile before serving. If you want a cheese ball, then roll in parsley flakes.

Italian Herbs

Italian herbs (which you can buy already mixed) are usually a blend of rosemary, marjoram, basil, and oregano; so you can mix your own using equal amounts, or you can play with the proportions to suit your taste.

I also use dry cilantro leaves, - use the oregano sparingly at first, as it is the most powerful of the seasonings. It is best to keep the garlic out of this mix, and add it separately, as well as salt (which is not to say you should not use garlic salt, as I use it a lot).

Black Bean Soup

1 pound black beans, washed and soaked overnight
one large Spanish sweet onion chopped
1 ½ cup chopped celery
1 cup chopped carrots
one chopped red bell pepper
large smoked fat ham hock or two smaller ones
Salt, pepper, and cumin to taste.
one gal chicken stock (or bullion cubes and 2 tablespoons olive oil)
1 cup raw rice
4 tablespoons dry wine - preferably red

Saute the vegetables in bacon drippings for about 10 minutes over medium heat. Drain the black beans from the soaking water; and add to the vegetables, and then add the chicken stock and ham hocks. Cook at a gentle boil for two to four hours (depending upon how long you have soaked the beans).

Cook beans until they are just soft; and add the rice, salt, pepper, and cumin. Cook until the rice is done — about 30 to 45 minutes — and add the wine, and adjust the seasonings.

> **Note:** If you don't have or don't wish to use wine, you can substitute *only two tablespoons of cider vinegar.*

You can also add a small can of whole kernel corn if desired.

Curry Chicken Salad with Melon

Salad:
You will need three melons and you can use any combination:

papaya, honeydew, cantaloupe, crenshaw, etc.
6 cups chopped skinless chicken breasts
or other parts
2 cups seedless grapes — try ½ green and ½ red
2 cups chopped celery
1 cup chopped water chestnuts.

Dressing:
8 ounces sour cream
4 ounces vanilla yogurt
1 ½ teaspoon curry powder

Mix the sour cream, yogurt and curry; and set aside while you assemble the salad.

Cut melons; remove seeds; and scoop out melon balls. Reserve the melon rinds for "serving bowls". If you don't want to make melon balls or if you can't find the scoop, then just cut up the melon into small cubes, and serve the salad on a lettuce leaf.

Toss together the melon balls, chicken, celery, grapes, and water chestnuts. Then gently toss the salad with the dressing, and add salt and fresh ground pepper to taste.

Things You Need.

Let's spend a few minutes talking about cookware — pots and pans. With the exception of the fact that I MUST have my cast iron skillet, I use Revere Ware; and I don't think you can get better cookware.

There is a lot of designer cookware out there today, as well as the door to door or home party sale cookware; but I think it is over priced, and although the claims made are not false...*they just do not make any difference in your cooking.*

Now this is my opinion, and if you merely want something to "go with" your kitchen, then have at it; but, if not, go to a large department store or discount house and get your Revere Ware.. I presume that this steps on some toes, but I want you to cook good food and do so without spending money unnecessarily.

Remember: *"Waste Not - Want Not"*

Grrrreat Flake Bars

1 - 10 ounce package Frosted Flakes
1 - 10 ounce package marshmallows
⅓ cup margarine
⅓ cup crunchy peanut butter
a well buttered 9x13 pyrex dish

In a large saucepan, melt margarine; and add marshmallows, and stir until melted. Then add peanut butter, and mix until smooth. Add flakes and toss, until fully coated.

Turn mixture into pyrex pan and press down with buttered fingers. Cool and cut into squares. And yes, you can make with Rice Krispies; and you can leave out the peanut butter, but try these; and you will have a new treat. You will also make some "Tiger" happy!

Green Potato Soup

2 large Irish potatoes and 1 large sweet potato, peeled and cubed
1 - 12 ounce package frozen green peas
6 cups chicken stock (or bullion from cubes)
1 teaspoon dried dill weed crushed
⅛ teaspoon cayenne pepper
1 large onion, minced
and 2 Tablespoons olive oil

Put onion in large saucepan with oil, and cook until clear. Add Irish and sweet potatoes, the seasonings, and the stock; and boil until the potatoes are just done. Then add the green peas, and cook about 15 minutes longer.

Puree the soup in a food processor, and return to saucepan. Add Vege-Sal and fresh ground pepper to taste, and serve. If you prefer, place a teaspoon sour cream in the center of each filled bowl, and sprinkle a few chives over the sour cream. (Note that you do this just as you are serving, or the cream will start to melt, which it is going to do anyway; but you obviously want to serve before it does).

This soup has a wonderful flavor, but don't tell people what it is until after they have eaten it; for sometimes people flinch just from the name, and they prejudge the flavor. If they ask, *"what is this . . . ?"*, say *"just try it, and see how good it is.*

Hershey Dream

CRUST:

Spray a 9" springform with Baker's Joy. On a floured board, roll out a package of dairy case sugar cookie dough to fit the pie pan; and press into pie pan. Bake according to directions, until just light golden — do not let it get too brown.

FILLING:

1 - 6 ounce Hershey Bar, melted
8 ounce cream cheese
½ cup sugar
1 teaspoon vanilla
1 envelope Knox unflavored gelatin
2 cups whipping cream, whipped and divided
(reserve ½ of whipped cream for topping)

For some reason it seems that when you whip 2 cups, you get more than when you whip 2 - 1 cup portions separately; so whip both cups, and divide and put ½ of the whipped cream in separate container. Cover, and refrigerate for topping later.

This is best made with a stand up mixer. Beat together cream cheese, sugar, and vanilla, until smooth; then beat in melted Hershey. Put water in small saucepan; sprinkle the gelatin over the water, and let it stand for about a minute. Then turn on low heat, and stir until gelatin is dissolved.

Now, with mixer running on low speed, pour gelatin into chocolate. Fold in ½ half of your whipped cream, and spread into your crust. Put into refrigerator for about a hour; spread the remaining whipped cream on top, and serve.

Pizza Pie

Spray a 9x13 pyrex pan with Pam. Preheat Oven to 375°.

FILLING:

1 ½ pound ground beef
1 large onion, minced finely
½ teaspoon garlic salt
¼ teaspoon oregano
½ pound grated Mozzarella cheese.
1 16 ounce jar pizza sauce
½ pound fresh sliced mushrooms
sauted in margarine.

Brown meat in large skillet; add onion, and cook over medium heat until onion is soft. Add salt, oregano, and pizza sauce; mix well, and pour into pyrex pan. Add layer of mushrooms, and sprinkle Mozzarella over meat mixture.

CRUST:

1 cup flour
2 tablespoons soft margarine
2 eggs
1 cup milk
½ teaspoon Vege-Sal
½ cup fresh grated Parmesan cheese.

Mix salt and flour together, and cut in margarine until it is crumbly. Add milk and eggs (the dough mix will be soupy); then pour over casserole, and sprinkle the Parmesan on the top. Bake for 30 to 40 minutes.

New Potato Salad

1 pound tiny new potatoes, washed and quartered
2 cups fresh pea pods, sliced on bias
½ cup plain yogurt
½ cup mayonnaise
1 teaspoon crushed dill weed
1 tablespoon snipped chives
Fresh ground pepper
one head leaf lettuce.

Cook potatoes in boiling water for about 10 minutes; add pea pods, and cook 3 to 4 minutes longer. Drain in colander, and let cool while you make dressing.

Mix together the yogurt, mayonnaise, dillweed, chives and pepper. Toss with potatoes and peas, and refrigerate about ½ hour.

Then serve on lettuce leaves. You can sprinkle a little paprika on top to add color to this salad.

Crabmeat Cocktail

1 pound cooked flaked crabmeat
1 avocado diced
3 green onions, very finely sliced
½ bunch cilantro, chopped
2 limes
1 small cucumber, sliced thinly
Fresh ground pepper
1 bottle of Del Monte cocktail sauce
½ teaspoon Tabasco

Toss everything together, except the cocktail sauce; and squeeze the lime juice over the salad. Refrigerate for about 1 hour or more.

Add Tabasco to the cocktail sauce, and shake. Serve the crab with the cocktail sauce on the side. This is really Ceviche. Even those who don't really like Ceviche will certainly like this...

You can serve this over slices of Beefsteak Tomatoes.

Steak Sauce

1 large onion, very very finely chopped
½ cup olive oil
½ cup red wine vinegar
½ cup water
1 ½ Tablespoons brown sugar
2 Tablespoons Worcestershire
½ teaspoon garlic powder
½ teaspoon oregano
½ teaspoon Lawry's salt
¼ teaspoon ground clove
2 teaspoon chili powder

Put onion and oil in sauce pan over low heat; and cook slow, until the onion is soft. Mash up the onion with a metal spoon; then add the remaining ingredients; and cook over medium heat for about 20 to 30 minutes, stirring frequently. Let the sauce get cool before pouring into jar. Keep unused portion in refrigerator.

Thinking is the hardest work there is, which is the probable reason why so few engage in it.
—Henry Ford

X1X

In the book of life — the answers are not in the back of the book.
— Charlie Brown

Broccoli Cornbread

2 packages Jiffy Cornbread Mix
1 package frozen chopped broccoli
4 eggs
½ pound margarine
1 cup small curd cottage cheese
9 X 13 pyrex sprayed with Baker's Joy

Cook broccoli according to package directions, and drain well. Place margarine in warm mixing bowl so that it melts to a very soft stirring consistency. (You can set in warm oven). First, beat in cottage cheese, and then eggs.

Pour in cornbread mix, and mix well. Stir in broccoli. Pour into pyrex pan, and bake at 350° until golden brown, about 20 minutes. Cut in pan, and serve; or you can cut in small squares and serve as an appetizer.

Authentic Caesar Salad

To make a true Caesar Salad, you will need a wooden bowl and a wooden spoon; because mashing the garlic and anchovies to a smooth paste is the secret to success.

1 clove garlic
6 anchovy fillets
dash of salt
1 teaspoon Worcestershire
½ teaspoon Dijon mustard
1 egg yolk
the juice of 2 lemons, strained
½ cup olive oil
a large bunch romaine lettuce
2 tablespoons fresh grated Parmesan cheese
a skillet of garlic flavored croutons (See below)

Put a dash of salt into your wooden bowl, and rub the garlic clove into the salt and all around the bowl. Then add the anchovies, and mash the anchovies and garlic into a smooth paste with your wooden spoon. Next beat in the Worcestershire, mustard, and egg yolk; and whip well. Now add the lemon juice, a little at a time to keep mixed, and finally the olive oil, whipping all the time. Add lettuce, and toss to coat with dressing. Sprinkle the Parmesan and croutons over salad, and toss again to coat every thing well with the dressing.

Home Made Garlic Croutons
⅓ cup olive oil
1 clove garlic sliced
3 slices light bread
2 tablespoons fresh grated Parmesan

Trim crust from bread, and cut into squares. (You can use any type of bread —brown, pumpernickel, rye, etc. — but white is what I prefer for Caesar).

Heat oil in skillet with garlic until garlic begins to brown. Remove garlic; add the bread, and quickly toss to coat with oil. Fry until the bread is golden; then remove skillet from heat, and toss the croutons with 2 tablespoons fresh grated Parmesan.

Alabama Corn Casserole

1 can cream style corn
1 cup Bisquick mix
1 egg
2 tablespoons olive oil
½ cup milk
a small can whole green chilies
1 ½ cup grated Monterey Jack or Co-Jack cheese

Prepare a 2 quart casserole by spraying with Pam. In large mixing bowl, beat together the corn, biscuit mix, oil, egg, and milk. Pour ½ mixture into casserole, and spread green chilies over the mix.

Then cover the chilies with grated cheese, and cover with the remaining corn mixture. Bake at 325° for about 45 to 50 minutes, or until the top is a light golden brown. Do not get it too brown or the cheese will get tough; so check at about 35 minutes, and keep a good watch.

"Baked" Eggs With Hash

6 eggs
6 pats margarine
6 tablespoons milk
1 ½ pounds canned corn beef or roast beef hash

You need a skillet with a tight fitting lid for this.

Spread hash in skillet; and make six depressions, using the bottom of a glass or custard cup. Put a pat of margarine in each depression; break an egg in each depression, and put a tablespoon of milk over each egg. Cover skillet; and place on low heat for about 20 minutes, or until eggs are set. Grind a bit of fresh pepper over the eggs, and serve.

Brandied Mixed Fruit Spread

12 ounces dried mixed fruit (or you may use
peaches or apricots, alone)
1 cup sugar
15 ounce can crushed pineapple
2 tablespoons brandy

Put dry fruit and sugar into sauce pan, and spread out evenly. Add just enough water to barely cover.

Cook on medium heat, stirring often until the mixture starts to thicken (this will take about 30 minutes). Add the pineapple; cook about 10 minutes longer, and stir in the brandy. This will make about 2 pints; which you will need to refrigerate and use within 30 days in that there is no preservative in this. It is great on hot biscuits.

Louisiana Boiled Shrimp

1 pound raw shrimp
1 can beer
1 stick cinnamon
4 cloves, whole
1 teaspoon seasoning salt

Empty beer into sauce pan, and add three cans of water and all seasonings. Bring to a rolling boil, and dump in shrimp. Remove from heat, and let stand for about five minutes.

Check shrimp for doneness, and then add ice cubes to cool quickly and stop cooking process. (Note that over cooked shrimp are tough).

New Orleans Style Shrimp Sauce

1 cup mayonnaise
3 tablespoons fresh grated horseradish
1 tablespoon capers
paprika

Mix mayonnaise, horseradish, and capers together, and sprinkle paprika over top. Let chill in refrigerator for about 20 minutes.

You should make the sauce before you cook the shrimp.

This sauce is also great on a char-broiled steak.

Neiman Marcus Spiced Tea

There are a lot of good flavored teas, but this one is similar to the early Neiman Marcus version, which I first tasted in the old Garden Court at North Park Mall in Dallas. Its distinction is in the use of Almond extract. Although I have varied and modified this recipe throughout the years, I will give you the one I prefer and now use:

1 gallon size Nestea Iced Tea bag
1 gallon boiling hot water
½ teaspoon cinnamon
½ teaspoon nutmeg
1 teaspoon Almond Extract
6 or 7 whole cloves
¾ cup orange Tang

Boil water; and while water is coming to a boil, fill a gallon jar with hot tap water to warm jar.(This will prevent the boiling water from cracking the jar — I hope).

When water has come to a boil, empty the jar; and add cinnamon, nutmeg, and cloves to the jar. Place the jar in the sink, and fill with the boiling water, leaving just enough room to put in the tea bag. Hold one corner of the tea bag and put just the corner of the bag over the rim of the jar in order that the lid will hold the bag and not allow it to fall down into the jar.

Set the jar on a trivet, and let the tea brew until the jar is cool to touch —6 to 7 hours. Then remove the tea bag, and add the Tang and Almond Extract. Refrigerate several hours before serving. Use large ice cubes in order not to dilute the tea when serving.

XX

It has been said that great cooks are born, not made; and to some extent this may be true, but to be a *GOOD* cook, you need not be enshrined as one of the great cooks. The love of food and family will make you a good cook, and the simple fact that you care enough to do your very best.

I do not believe that all men (or women) are created equal; I believe that the differences are what we enjoy and appreciate. How can you say that a Robin is more beautiful than a Bluebird, as each has its own beauty and neither detracts from the other. Soul Food comes from the internal and not the external qualities of the person who is preparing the food. It is the love within that makes a good cook. Even though preparation has been speeded, I am sure that many of you reading this cookbook remember going to a family dinner where your Grandmother, Great-Aunt, etc. had cooked for days, preparing many dishes that she "knew" Bobby, Frank, Sue, or Linda, considered a favorite. To me, this is what makes a great cook.

Cook with this in mind, and feel the love spreading through the room at meal times.

Pico de Terry

3 large tomatoes, chopped
1 large red onion (at least a lb.)
1 4 ounce can chopped ripe olives
1 small can chopped green chilies
4 to 6 fresh cortina peppers, chopped
½ bunch cilantro, chopped
½ teaspoon garlic salt
½ teaspoon cracked black pepper
4 tablespoons olive oil

Combine all ingredients, and refrigerate overnight before serving. Keep unused portion refrigerated; this will not keep for more than a week in that there is no vinegar in this to act as a preservative

It is the absence of vinegar that gives this a special flavor.

A hamburger on a toasted onion bun with Jarlsberg cheese, mayonnaise, and Pico de Terry is without equal.

When you have eaten all the pico and only have juice, then pour the juice into a sauce pan; and add 2 cups of white great northern beans and about a quart of water. Cook your beans with this juice to flavor the beans, adding only a little salt to taste.

Swiss Steak

¼ cup flour
1 teaspoon salt
1 teaspoon fresh ground pepper
2 pounds round steak trimmed, and cut into strips
3 tablespoons olive oil
1 large onion chopped fine
1 cup chopped celery
1 cup chopped yellow bell pepper (you can use other peppers, according to taste)
1 large can tomatoes
(use kitchen shears to cut up in can)
2 cups water

Combine flour, salt, and pepper; and dredge meat in flour. Pound the flour in to both tenderize meat and coat well.

Heat oil in large deep skillet with a lid, and brown meat on both sides. Pour in the remaining ingredients, and reduce heat to low; so it will just simmer for an hour.

Check the meat with a fork, and cover and cook until tender. Then uncover, and cook about 15 minutes longer to thicken the sauce.

This is great served over white rice; and, with a salad, you have a complete meal.

Jarlsberg Tuna Melt

1 can water packed tuna
2 tablespoons sweet pickle relish
3 - 5 tablespoons mayonnaise
5 slices sandwich size Swiss Cheese (I like Jarlsberg)
10 slices sandwich bread
margarine

Drain and flake tuna; mix with relish and enough mayonnaise to make a spread. Heat skillet (Teflon, if you have it). Butter one side of each slice of bread; then spread the other side with tuna, and cover with cheese and the remaining bread (butter side up). Toast each sandwich until golden brown. You can make this with french, or sour dough bread if you prefer.

Cattleman's Meatloaf

1 pound lean ground beef
1 pound ground pork sausage
¾ cup 3 minute oatmeal
1 teaspoon Lawry's Salt
½ teaspoon fresh ground pepper
1 small onion, chopped finely
1 small can V-8 juice (about 4 ounce)
¼ cup picante sauce
2 tablespoons Worcestershire
1 egg

Mix all ingredients very thoroughly; then pack into a loaf pan; push it down tightly; and let it sit for 5 minutes in order for all the juice to be absorbed.

Turn out of loaf pan onto a rack of a roasting pan, and bake covered at 325° for 1 hour. About 15 minutes before the meatloaf is done, you can pour catsup over the top if desired. Serve with mashed potatoes, brown gravy and buttered yellow squash.

Quick Brown Gravy

1 can Franco-American brown or mushroom gravy
1 small can mushrooms pieces and stems, drained
1 small onion, chopped finely
3 tablespoons margarine
¼ cup dry red wine
1 tablespoon A-1 steak sauce
1 teaspoon fresh ground pepper
½ teaspoon salt

Saute the onion and mushrooms in margarine. Then add remaining ingredients, and cook until bubbly. Let simmer 2 to 3 minutes.

Buttered Yellow Squash

1 ½ pound yellow squash
a pot of boiling water with
1 teaspoon salt and 1 tablespoon milk
butter

Wash and slice the squash in thick slices, and put into boiling water. Cook until tender — about 5 minutes. Remove pan from stove, and drain off water. Leave squash in pan; and add about ¼ cup butter, cut in pats so it melts quickly in the hot squash. I like a little fresh ground pepper on this.

S.O.S. was a common WWII term used to describe the Army version of chipped beef, but thank goodness, it is no longer applicable to the chipped beef of today.

The final "S" in S.O.S. refers to dry unbuttered toast, and is not at all what I would recommend. The following recipe for *"S.O."* will be a pleasant surprise over noodles.

Chipped Beef

1 jar dry beef, cut into small pieces
½ cup margarine (equally divided into 2 portions)
3 teaspoons flour
2 cups milk
1 teaspoon fresh ground pepper

Put beef in skillet with ¼ cup margarine, and fry until it is just crisp. Add flour, and stir to mix well — no lumps. Add the remaining margarine; and when it is melted and the mix is smooth, slowly add the milk and the pepper. Keep stirring until the milk is bubbly and the gravy is creamy; add milk to thin as necessary.

Serve over noodles.

For variation, add a finely chopped onion when you fry the beef. And for a really great dish, add a chopped banana pepper and ½ cup chopped fresh mushrooms.

The Army was never like this.

A Little Knowledge Helps

This is a really important hint: When you have finished cooking your vegetables, especially beans, it is OK to leave them covered for a few minutes before serving; but - *never leave covered while cooling to room temperature*. Vegetables tend to sour when cooling in a covered pot.

So, as Mama would say: *"never leave your hat on in the house"*, which is to say, *"cook covered and refrigerate covered, but **leave uncovered when bringing to room temperature.**"* Always let your food cool to room temperature before putting in refrigerator.

Richard's Unconventional Breakfast

In oversize cup, put 1 ½ envelope of Nestles hot cocoa mix and a hand full of marshmallows. Pour in boiling water, and stir until marshmallows melt.

Split an onion bun, and lightly butter; toast in skillet and set aside. Place a double size sausage patty in skillet, and press out to bun size. Add a slice of onion while cooking sausage. When sausage is brown on one side, turn and put onion on top; and cover with swiss cheese. Turn off burner. Sausage will continue to brown, and cheese will melt. Put top of onion roll on sausage, and spread mustard on bottom.

Since you have finished your hot chocolate while cooking, you will need a Dr. Pepper with your sausage sandwich.

Dessert Rice

1 ½ cup brown rice
4 cups water
1 teaspoon salt
1 tablespoon margarine
1 cup raisins (You don't need to plump these)
½ cup honey
1 ½ to 2 teaspoons cinnamon

Bring water to boil; and add rice, salt and margarine. Reduce heat to low, and cover and cook about 30 minutes until water is absorbed and rice is tender. Stir in honey and sprinkle cinnamon on top.

You can serve with a little milk over each serving, if desired. This also makes a great hot breakfast dish on a cold morning.

Hot Buttered Pears

1 can pear halves, cut into quarters
¼ cup margarine
3 tablespoons dark brown sugar

Melt margarine in skillet; add brown sugar, and stir until dissolved. Place pears in skillet, and gently stir to coat all fruit with margarine. Cook on low until pears are hot, and sauce is slightly thickened.

There are many ways to use this recipe: as a side dish, over Dessert Rice, or along side roast pork. You can also substitute apples for the pears.

XXI

The Diamond T Ranch, a 187 acre spread in Hunt County, Texas, is my retreat from the city and also a place which has had several lifetimes worth of work in order to make it shine. A recent visitor looking at this country paradise said, *"God has given you a most beautiful place."* To which my friend J. R. Gray replied, *"Yes, but you should have seen the condition it was in when He gave it to us."*

Morning Spiced Hot Cider

One envelope Alpine Instant Spiced Cider
10 to 12 Cinnamon Red Hots

Put in large mug, and pour in boiling hot water. Stir, let sit for a few minutes; and stir again until red hots are melted.

Diamond T Spiced Apple Juice

one large jar (64 ounces) apple juice
one small package red hots
one cinnamon stick
4 whole cloves

Open jar, and remove ½ cup juice (drink straight). Add red hots, cinnamon, and cloves to the jar.

Refrigerate for three days. Shake jar at least three times per day to melt the red hots and mix the flavors.

You can serve this hot or cold. If you want it hot, then you need not refrigerate it for three days. Just add ingredients, and heat until the red hots are melted.

French Toast

2 eggs
½ cup half and half
a sprinkle of salt
3 slices light bread
2 tablespoons Unsalted butter
Powdered sugar

Preheat both oven and teflon coated cookie sheet to 350°.

Beat together eggs, half & half (or heavy cream if you desire extra richness), and salt.

Heat butter in skillet (not too high of heat, as you don't want to brown the butter). Cut the bread in half, and dredge in the egg mix to coat completely. Fry toast until golden, and place in oven to crisp for about 4 to 5 minutes.

Sprinkle with powdered sugar, and serve with syrup or jam.

Lemon - Cream Cheese Pound Cake

1 ½ cups lightly salted butter or margarine
8 ounces cream cheese
6 eggs
1 tablespoon vanilla
*the rind of a good size lemon, grated on a fine sieve
the juice from the lemon, strained
3 cups sugar
3 cups flour, sifted with 1 tablespoon baking powder
bundt pan (preferably teflon), with Baker's Joy

Bring butter and cream cheese to room temperature, and cream together. Add eggs, one at a time, mixing well after each egg. Next add vanilla, lemon juice and rind; and mix well.

Stir in sugar until well blended; add flour, and mix well. Pour into bundt pan, and bake at 350° for about 1 hour and 15 minutes. Straw test to see if done.

Cool in pan for 10 to 12 minutes. Then invert onto plate, and cool completely.

You can also make this with an orange, using all the rind, but only about 2 tablespoons of the juice (or in place of the orange juice, use 2 tablespoons Meyers Rum).

And if you would like a vanilla cake, then skip the fruit and use 2 tablespoons vanilla.

Or try 1 teaspoon vanilla and 2 tablespoons of either Meyers Dark Rum or Chambrod.

Pineapple Right-Side-Up Cake

2 cups flour, self-rising type
2 cups sugar
1 tablespoon vanilla
1 egg
¼ cup oil
1 20 ounce can crushed pineapple with juice
9x13 pyrex prepared with Bakers Joy

In large bowl, mix all ingredients to a smooth batter; and pour into pyrex.

Bake at 375° for 35 to 40 minutes, and cool in pan.

A GOOD ICING

½ cup butter
⅔ cup Pet milk (canned evaporated)
1 cup sugar

Put all ingredients in a sauce pan, and bring to a boil on med heat. Boil for 3 to 4 minutes; then remove from stove.

Using ice pick or similar object, prick holes in top of cake — lots of holes.

Then pour icing over top of cake.

This is a great dessert to take somewhere; as it is all in its own dish, and very easy to prepare.

"Coke" Cake

This is a real "kid" pleaser, but be wary if the adults find it.

2 cups flour
2 cups sugar
1 cup margarine
1 cup Coca Cola or Cherry Coke
1 tablespoon Hershey's cocoa
½ cup buttermilk
2 eggs
1 teaspoon baking soda
¼ teaspoon salt
1 ½ cup miniature marshmallows
(use colored ones if you like)
a 9x13 pyrex prepared with Bakers Joy

Sift flour and sugar into large mixing bowl. In a sauce pan, heat coke and the cocoa to boiling; then pour into flour, and beat until smooth. Add buttermilk, eggs, baking soda, and vanilla; and mix well. Stir in marshmallows - it is OK if they float to the top. Pour batter into pyrex, and bake at 350° for 35 minutes.

This cake should be *iced white still hot;* so prepare icing while cake is baking.

½ cup margarine
⅓ cup Coke or Cherry Coke
2 tablespoons cocoa
1 pound powdered sugar
1 teaspoon vanilla
1 cup pecan pieces to garnish top

Nuts are optional; some "kids" like the cake better without the nuts; but they are a must for most adults.

Heat the margarine, Coke, and cocoa in a 2 quart sauce pan until it comes to a boil; and remove from heat. Add the powdered sugar and vanilla, and whip until creamy smooth. Then spread over the hot cake, which is fresh from the oven. Garnish with pecans if desired.

Spinach In Sour Cream

1 pound spinach, cooked and drained
(fresh, frozen or canned)
½ cup finely chopped onion,
cooked clear in 2 tablespoons margarine
½ cup sour cream
½ teaspoon Lawry's Salt
½ teaspoon fresh ground pepper
8x8 pyrex, prepared with Pam

Mix all ingredients, and turn into pyrex. Bake at 350° for about 25 minutes, or until bubbly hot.

Salmon Croquettes

1-15 ounce can salmon
1 small onion, chopped very finely
½ cup very finely chopped celery
½ cup cracker crumbs (any kind of crackers, or corn, or bran flakes or a mix, or even potato chips)
a heaping tablespoon mayonnaise
2 eggs
1 teaspoon Worcestershire
½ teaspoon fresh ground pepper or more
Olive oil

Mix all ingredients in a large bowl, adding an extra egg if necessary in order for the mixture to be the right consistency to form patties. Shape patties in hands, using about ⅓ cup of mixture for each.

Heat about an inch of olive oil in a skillet — preferably a cast iron one — and fry patties until golden brown.

True Beef Stroganoff

2 pounds sirloin steak,
trimmed and cut into finger size strips
½ cup unsalted butter
2 cups fresh mushroom slices
1 medium onion, chopped
1 can cream of mushroom soup
¼ cup half and half
¼ cup dry red wine
3 beef bullion cubes (melted in red wine above)
1 teaspoon Lawry's Salt
1 teaspoon cracked pepper
¼ teaspoon nutmeg
1 cup sour cream

In a large deep skillet, melt butter over medium heat; and add meat, mushrooms and onion. Cook with lid on until steak is done and onions tender. Add all remaining ingredients, except sour cream; and simmer again with lid on — about 25-30 minutes — stirring every few minutes to keep smooth. Just before serving, stir in the sour cream. Serve over egg noodles.

This same recipe can be used with 1 ½ pound ground beef, cooked to crumbly and drained.

Southern Baked Pork Cutlets

½ cup milk
1 egg
1 teaspoon fresh ground pepper
1 ½ cup crushed corn flakes or rice krispies
1 green onion chopped including top
1 teaspoon Adkins Dry Bar B Q Mix
¼ teaspoon garlic powder
¼ cup margarine
4 pork cutlets

Melt margarine in 8x8 pyrex.

Mix milk, egg, and pepper in dish to dip cutlets.

On a plate, mix corn flakes, onion, Adkins, and garlic.

Take coated cutlets from egg mix; dredge in corn flakes, and then place in pyrex. After all cutlets are in pyrex, turn once so that both sides are buttered.

Bake at 350° for 45 minutes.

You can use pork chops for this recipe, but it takes a little longer for them to cook — about one hour total time, instead of 45 minutes.

You've got to love what's lovable, and hate what's hatable. It takes brains to see the difference.

— Robert Frost

XXII

Neiman - Marcus Poppy Seed Dressing

This is a Helen Corbitt recipe, and it is one which I don't think has had any change over the years.

You'll need fresh onion juice, which can be made by putting a *white* onion in a blender and blending to pulp and then straining to capture the juice.

1 ½ cup sugar
2 teaspoon dry mustard
2 teaspoon salt
⅔ cup white vinegar
3 tablespoons fresh prepared onion juice
2 cups Crisco Vegetable or Corn oil (not olive oil)
3 tablespoons poppy seeds

In a blender, mix the vinegar, sugar, salt, and mustard. Then with blender running, pour the oil in, using a very slow stream. Continue to beat until thick; then add the poppy seeds, and blend a few minutes longer. Pour into a jar; and if you are going to use for the meal today, you can put the jar on the counter in a cool place until mealtime. If you need to store, then put in the door of the refrigerator -in the warmest part, as the dressing will separate if it gets too cold (or too hot).

Eagle Brand Fudge

1 -11 ½ ounce pkg. milk chocolate morsels
1 -16 ounce pkg. semi sweet morsels
1 can Eagle Brand Sweet Condensed milk
1 teaspoon vanilla
1 cup chopped pecans or walnuts or Spanish peanuts

Melt morsels in double boiler; when all are melted, add remaining ingredients.

Line a 9x12 pyrex with wax paper; pour mixture into pyrex, and refrigerate until firm. Cut, and keep in refrigerator.

Easy Potatoes Au Gratin

1 16 ounce pkg shredded hash brown potatoes
1 can cream of potato soup
1 cup sour cream
1 ½ cups shredded American or Co-jack cheese
½ cup fresh grated Parmesan

Combine hash browns, soup, sour cream and 1 cup of the shredded cheese in bowl; and spoon into a 8x8 pyrex, prepared with Pam. Sprinkle the remaining shredded cheese on top, and then the Parmesan.

Bake at 350° for 30 to 40 minutes, watching to see that the top doesn't get too brown.

Serve with a pat of butter on each serving.

Traditional Tuna Salad

2 can water packed tuna, well drained and flaked
1 ½ cup mayonnaise
½ cup sweet pickle relish
1 small onion chopped (optional)
⅓ cup finely chopped celery
1 teaspoon parsley flakes
½ teaspoon celery salt
¼ teaspoon Vege-Sal
½ teaspoon black pepper
2 hard boiled eggs, grated on large grate

Mix all ingredients in food storage bowl with tight fitting lid. Cover, and refrigerate for about an hour before serving.

Kentucky Style Potato Salad

Skin and dice about 3 pounds red or white boiling potatoes; boil in salted water until tender. Remove from heat; pour into colander, and run cold water over the potatoes to cool and stop the cooking — this keeps the potatoes from going to mush.

Put cooled potatoes in large bowl and add:

1 cup mayonnaise
½ cup chopped celery
½ cup chopped red onion
¼ cup dill relish *
2 teaspoons Dijon mustard
2 teaspoon parsley flakes
½ teaspoon Vege-Sal
½ teaspoon fresh ground pepper

*All right, if you want sweet salad, use sweet relish. but it just isn't the same. If you can't find dill relish, then chop dill pickle finely.

Toss together to mix well, adding mayonnaise as required to make the salad creamy. Refrigerate if you are not serving within 15 minutes, but take the salad out about 15 minutes before serving; for it is best if it is not too cold.

Lillian's Salad

You'll need a large wooden salad bowl, seasoned with garlic. Cut a garlic in half, and place the cut side in the bowl. With the back of a fork, press the garlic; and rub the bowl. Discard the garlic when completed.

1 solid head of Iceberg lettuce (at least a pound)
2 ripe tomatoes, chopped
¾ cup chopped green olives with pimento
(may be Spanish type)
the strained juice of a lemon
1 teaspoon Vege-Sal
¾ cup olive oil
1 tablespoon sugar

Core, wash, and drain the lettuce well. Break into pieces in your wooden bowl. Add tomatoes and olives, and toss. Put lemon juice, salt, sugar, and oil into a pint jar; and shake until the salt and sugar are dissolved. Then pour onto salad, and toss. Let the salad sit for about 10 minutes, and serve with fresh ground pepper. {Note that the lettuce will slightly wilt, which is correct for this salad).

Muskogee Baked Chicken Legs

Watch the sale ads in the paper, and frequently you will see chicken leg quarters come on sale at a good price. Buy several packages, and freeze them until you need them.

Place a package of leg quarters, skin side up, in deep 10x15 alum roasting pan (no lid); and sprinkle with salt. Bake at 300° for about 1 ½ hours, or until chicken is done. Skin will be golden. Pour off liquid into jar for use as broth. The chicken is good hot or cold in lunches or as a midnight snack; or you can use the meat for a chicken salad, etc.

I really wanted the broth for the mushroom soup below, which is just not the same with canned broth.

Old Fashion Mushroom Soup

This recipe calls for two items which can be substituted - one is the chicken broth - see above, and the other is half and half, for which you can use milk - 2%, skim etc., BUT in actuality, *there is no substitute for the taste and texture of half and half.* and if you want the truly old fashion taste, you will have to use the real things.

A word about buying mushrooms: Look for bulk mushrooms and choose nice white ones without bruises and ones which are closed on the bottom (meaning that the brown ribs do not show); for these are the fresh ones. Mushrooms open up as they grow older.

½ pound fresh mushrooms
¼ cup margarine
1 small white onion chopped
2 cups chicken broth
¼ cup flour
1 teaspoon Vege-Sal
1 teaspoon parsley flakes
½ teaspoon cracked pepper
2 tablespoons dry sherry, optional
2 cups half & half

Wash, drain, and pat the mushrooms dry with a paper towel. Then slice very thin. In a 5 to 6 quart soup pot, cook onions in margarine until tender; but do not brown. Add mushrooms and sherry, and stir cook on low heat for about 7 to 8 minutes.

Put flour into a mixing bowl; and slowly beat in the chicken broth, mixing well to prevent any lumps. Pour this into mushrooms, and add the remaining ingredients. Cook with lid on pot over medium heat for about 30 minutes, keeping heat low enough for the soup to just barely bubble. Serve with *buttered baguette toast rounds.*

Buttered Baguette Toast Rounds

1 fresh French baguette (a nice long one)
Butter

Cut the bread straight across, so you get rounds. Butter one side, and place on baking sheet (preferably - teflon). Bake in oven at 300° for about 45 minutes to 1 hour, until the bread is crisp. *Do not over cook; for you do not want to brown the bread.*

Easy Broccoli Cheese Soup

*1 box frozen chopped broccoli,
cooked according to package directions.
1 can cream of chicken soup
¾ soup can of half & half
¼ cup margarine
½ teaspoon fresh ground pepper
¼ teaspoon onion powder
⅛ teaspoon cayenne pepper
1 cup Velveeta cheese*

Drain the broccoli after cooking. Add all the ingredients to the broccoli pot, and cook over med-low heat until soup is good and hot and cheese is melted. Note that there is no salt in the recipe in that Velveeta cheese is salty; so taste soup and add a little Vege-Sal if needed.

Hint: onions will draw moisture from potatoes when they are stored together, which will make the onions mold faster. Onions store best in a closet on a rack where they get air all around them.

Cream Gravy — White Sauce — Sausage Gravy — Etc.

Any time you fry meat, breaded or not, you can use the pan drippings for gravy. Just pour off all but about 3 tablespoons, being sure to save the meat crisps. Add 3 tablespoons flour, and stir the flour in the hot drippings until it is golden. Then add 1 cup milk and mix well; if gravy is too thick, add more milk. Salt and pepper to taste. *White Sauce* is basically the same.

White Sauce

3 tablespoons margarine
3 tablespoons flour
1 cup milk

Melt margarine in skillet, and stir in flour to make paste. Then add milk; and cook until bubbly, adding milk, salt, and pepper as required.

To the gravy or white sauce, you can add any combination of the following:

> 1 cup grated cheese — Cheddar, Swiss, Co-jack, Smoked, etc. (If you use cheese, add it before you *salt*, as many cheeses are salty.)

> 1 teaspoon lemon juice, 1 teaspoon onion, 1 grated hard cooked egg which, incidentally, is great over cooked spinach

> To white sauce, add a beaten egg yolk and 1 tablespoon mayonnaise, and serve with salmon patties, for example.

> 2 tablespoons horseradish, 1 tablespoon white vinegar, and 1 teaspoon dry mustard makes a wonderful sauce for steak.

> Crumble cooked patty sausage into gravy, and serve over biscuits or buttered noodles.

> Slice Echrich smoked sausage very thin, and serve over buttered noodles with white sauce.

These are only a few, but you can surely start thinking of combinations you would like to try.

Mother's Bread Puddin'

5 slices white bread cut into small pieces
1 cup whole milk
1- 7 ounce can Pet milk
¾ cup sugar
2 egg yolks, separated from 2 egg whites
(for meringue)
2 tablespoons melted margarine
1 teaspoon vanilla

Put bread into mixing bowl; and add milk, Pet Milk, sugar, egg yolks, and vanilla. Mix well; and pour into 8x8 pyrex (ungreased), and bake at 450° for 15 minutes.
Beat egg whites until stiff, and slowly add 2 tablespoons sugar. Spread meringue on top of pudding, and return to oven for approximately 5 minutes - until meringue is golden. Watch carefully in order not to burn the meringue.

Marinated Pork Chops

4 Butterfly pork chops
1 small can pineapple juice
¼ cup margarine
1 cup chutney
Vege-Sal and fresh ground pepper to taste

Sprinkle each chop with Vege-Sal and fresh ground pepper, and place in a glass dish (8x8 if they will lie flat, or 9x13 or whatever works to keep them close fitting). Pour pineapple juice over them; and marinate in refrigerator 24 hours, turning at mid point.

In large skillet, melt margarine on med heat; remove chops from marinade, and brown on each side. Then spread chutney over the chops, and pour enough marinade in to come up even with the top of the chops. Reduce heat, and simmer for 25 minutes.

A Different Green Bean Casserole

2 boxes frozen French sliced green beans
1-#303 can bean sprouts, drained
8 ounce can water chestnuts
½ pound fresh mushrooms, sliced
3 whole green onions, sliced including tops
1 cup grated cheese — Co-Jack or mild Cheddar type
2 cans cream of mushroom soup
1 can French fried onions

Let the green beans thaw. Using a 2 quart casserole make a layer with 1/2 the ingredients listed and in the order listed, except fried onions. Then repeat. Bake at 350° for 25 minutes. Put fried onion rings on top, and return to oven for about 15 minutes. Watch so onion rings do not get too brown.

We are shaped and fashioned by what we love
— Johann Wolfgang von Goethe

XXIII

As a parting word, I would like to thank you for reading this cookbook. I have had a great deal of enjoyment putting down my thoughts and recipes. It has brought back so many fond memories of food, fun, and family: happiness that has been shared by those whom I love and who loved me, and some wonderful giving. Some of those who gave to me are now gone from this earth; yet their love lives on and will continue to live in the pages of this book.

May the food you prepare reflect the feelings of your soul.

Mine does,

Richard F Thompson

Richard Ford Thompson

INDEX

Appetizers
 Crabmeat Cocktail, 173
 Louisiana Boiled Shrimp, 179
Artichokes
 Delicious Artichokes, 93
Avocados
 Summer Avocado Salad, 96
 Beans
 As Veggies, 14
 The Absolute Best
 Bar-B-Q Beans, 43
 Bean & Sausage Stew, 159
 Beans ... Beans ... Beans, 19
 Black Bean Soup, 166
 Cooking in Soup, 12
 Great Northern Beans, 87
 Pinto, with Chili, 18
 Red Beans, 19
Beef
 Cattleman's Meatloaf, 184
 Chipped Beef over Noodles, 186
 Mississippi Stir Fry Beef
  w/Greens, 51
 Mouth Watering Pot Roast, 92
 Pepper Beef Tenderloin, 57
 Roma Meat Roll, 103
 Swiss Steak, 183
 Texas Tortilla Casserole, 124
 True Beef Stroganoff, 195
 True Lasagna, 137
Breads
 After School Muffins, 65
 Baking Powder Bisquits, 158
 Bess's Rye Rolls, 107
 Breadstick Snacks, 69
 Breakfast Muffins, 31
 Broccoli Cornbread, 175
 Buttered Baguette Toast Rounds, 202
 Buttermilk Biscuits, 158
 Cranapple Muffins, 139
 Crumpets, 27
 Dumplings, 156
 French Toast, 190
 German Sweet Potato Bisquits, 1:
 Jalapeno Cornbread, 144
 Jiffy Cornbread, 15
 Nutty-Cheese Toast, 51
 Oatmeal Banana Nut Bread, 131
 Scones, 26
Broccoli
 Broccoli Cornbread, 175
 Broccoli Rice Casserole, 151
 Easy Broccoli Cheese Soup, 203
Brownies
 Eagle Brand Brownies, 128
 East Texas Brownies, 148
Brussel Sprouts
 Really Good Brussel Sprouts, 44
Butters
 Cashew Nut Butter, 134
 Chocolate Nut Butter, 149
 Virgina Honey Nut Butter, 134
Cabbage
 Cole-n-Sak, 74
 Cooked Cabbage, 44
Cakes
 Apple Spice Icebox Cake, 32
 Coco Loco Pound Cake, 82
 Coke Cake, 193
 Dorothy's Hummingbird Cake, ʃ
 Lemon Cream Cheese Pound Ca
 191
 Oatmeal Pound Cake, 55
 Old Time Chocolate Cake, 118
 Pineapple Right Side Up Cake, 1
 Pineapple Upside-Down Cake, 2
 Richard's Famous German Cho
 late Upside-Down Cake, 25

Sachertorte, 105
Savory Pound Cake, 23
Candy
Eagle Brand Fudge, 198
Grrrreat Flake Bars, 169
Peanut Brittle, 120
Penuche, 61
Rice Krispie Treats, 75
Carrots
Carrot Jell-o Salad, 46
Catalina Carrot Coins, 45
Cauliflower
Tender Cooked Cauliflower, 45
Cheese
Baked Parmesan Noodles, 102
Cheddar Dip, 119
Cheese Soup, 154
Chili con queso, 29
Curry Cheese Spread, 101
Jarlsberg Cheese Fondue, 53
Kentucky Cheese Torte, 50
Louisiana Cheese Crisps, 100
Mother's Hors d' oeuvres, 29
Noel's Swiss Cheese Ball, 132
Nutty-Cheese Toast, 51
Parmesan Cream Spread, 165
Richard's Cheese Sauce, 45
Smoked Turkey Ball, 129
Chicken
Alabama Mushroom Chicken, 148
Cheesie Chicken Casserole, 86
Chicken in Plantation Sauce, 108
Chicken Pie Especial, 85
Curry Chicken Salad w/ Melon, 167
Hunter's Chicken or
Chicken Cacciatore, 36
Left Over Chicken, 79
Muskogee Chicken Legs, 201
Potpourri Jambalaya, 99
Poultry Plus, 35
White Folks' Chicken, 36
Chili
About Chilies, 17
Beef Chili, 18
Chili con queso, 29
Chili for One, 17
Chili Rice, 150
Richard's Chili, 64
Sonora Chili, 17
Cookies
Almond Crescents, 115
Coconut Raisin Oatmeal , 125
Gingerbread Cookies, 69
Old Fashioned Sand Tarts, 60
Shortbread Cookies, 59
Cooking Tips
A Little Knowledge Helps, 187
Chopping Onions without Tears, 114
Eliminating Odors, 114
Helpful Hints, 113
Soften Sugar the Easy Way, 114
Test for Doneness, 113
Things You Need, 168
What To Do If It's Too Salty, 114
Corn
Alabama Corn Casserole, 177
Alabama Corn Patties, 46
Corn Relish, 143
Escalloped Corn, 47
Oven Roastin' Corn, 46
Tennessee Corn Casserole, 130
Crab
Crabmeat Cocktail, 173
Desserts
Almond Crescents, 115
Apple Spice Icebox Cake, 32
Banana Cream Pie, 33
Bread Pudding, 62
Butterscotch Bars, 126
Chocolate Icebox Pie, 123
Coco-Loco Pound Cake, 82
Coconut Cream Pie, 34
Coconut Raisin Oatmeal, 125
Coke Cake, 193
Cream Cheese Pie, 147
Cream Puff Ring, 54
Dessert Rice, 188
Dorothy's Hummingbird Cake, 81
Eagle Brand Brownies, 128

Eagle Brand Fudge, 198
East Texas Brownies, 148
French Silk Pie, 101
German Chocolate Pie, 128
Gingerbread Cookies, 69
Grrrreat Flake Bars, 169
Hershey Bar Pie, 112
Hershey Dream, 170
Hot Buttered Pears, 188
Key Lime Pie, 127
Krazy Apple Krisp, 145
Lemon Cream Cheese Pound Cake, 191
Mother's Bread Puddin', 205
Oatmeal Pound Cake, 55
Old Fashioned Sand Tarts, 60
Old Time Chocolate Cake, 118
Pecan Pie . . . etc., 48
Penuche, 61
Pineapple Right-Side-Up Cake, 192
Pineapple Upside-Down Cake, 24
Popcorn Puddin', 68
Pot d' Creme — Egg Custard — Flan', etc., 83
Pumpkin Pie, 87
Raisin Corn Puddin', 22
Rice Krispie Treats, 75
Richard's German Chocolate Upside-Down Cake, 25
Sacher Torte, 105
Savory Pound Cake, 23
Shortbread Cookies, 59
Strawberry Icebox Pie, 123
Strawberry Pie, 116
Would Anybody Like Some Pie?, 32

Dressing
Stuffing, 38

Drinks
Diamond T Spiced Apple Juice, 189
Morning Spiced Hot Cider, 189
Neiman Marcus Spiced Tea, 180

Dumplings, 156
Cornmeal Dumplings, 133

Eggs
Baked Eggs with Hash, 178
French Toast, 190

Entrees
Alabama Mushroom Chicken, 14
Baked Eggs with Hash, 178
Baked Ham Hash, 157
Barbequed Spam, 31
Bean and Sausage Stew, 159
Kentucky Cheese Torte, 50
Cattleman's Meatloaf, 184
Cheesie Chicken Casserole, 86
Chicken Fried Steak, 63
Chicken in Plantation Sauce, 108
Chicken Pie Especial, 85
Chipped Beef — not S.O.S., 186
Crustless Quiche, 153
Dallas Jambalaya, 77
Easy Salmon Patties, 78
Easy Tuna Casserole, 67
Escalloped Pork Chops, 75
French Toast, 190
Hunter's Chicken or Chicken Caciatore, 36
Italian Sausage, 78
Jarlsberg Tuna Melt, 184
Left Over Chicken, 79
Marinated Pork Chops, 205
Mississippi Stir Fry Beef w/Green 51
Mouth Watering Pot Roast, 92
Muskogee Baked Chicken Leg 201
My Mama's Hot Quiche, 110
Padre Island Shrimp Roast, 96
Pepper Beef Tenderloin, 57
Pizza Pie, 171
Potpourri Jambalaya, 99
Poultry Plus, 35
Rack of Spam, 30
Richard's Chili, 64
Roma Meat Roll, 103
Salmon Croquettes, 194
Smothered Baked Potatoes, 58
South Texas Pork Stew, 76

Southern Baked Pork Cutlets, 196
Swiss Steak, 183
Tamale Pie, 163
Tamales, 161
Texas Tortilla Casserole, 124
The Original Breakfast Tacos, 42
True Beef Stroganoff, 195
True Lasagna, 137
White Folks' Chicken, 36

sh
Crabmeat Cocktail, 173
Dallas Jambalaya, 77
Easy Salmon Patties, 78
Easy Tuna Casserole, 67
Louisiana Boiled Shrimp, 179
Marinated Shrimp, 97
Padre Island Shrimp Roast, 96
Salmon Croquettes, 194
The World's Best Tuna Salad, 21

ndues
Jarlsberg Cheese Fondue, 53

ostings
A Good Icing, 192
Chocolate Icing, 119
Coke Icing, 193
Cream Cheese Frosting, 82

avy
Cream Gravy—White Sauce—Sausage Gravy, etc., 203
Gravy for One, 10
Pan Gravy from Pork Roast, 9
Quick Brown Gravy, 185

een Beans
Different Green Bean Casserole, 206
Green Bean Bundles, 95
Green Bean Casserole I, 116
Green Bean Casserole II, 117
Green Bean Casserole III, 117
Spanish Green Beans, 146

its
Missippi Cheese Grits, 111

Hors d' oeurves
Pigs -n- Blanket, 41

Hors d' oeuvres
Breadstick Snacks, 69
Caviar Spread, 122
Cheddar Dip, 119
Chili con queso, 29
Curry Cheese Spread, 101
Ham & Cheese Rollups, 140
Jarlsberg Cheese Foundue, 53
Louisiana Cheese Crisps, 100
Marinated Shrimp, 97
Melba's Garlic Sweet Pickles, 141
Mother's Hors d' oeuvres, 29
Noel's Swiss Cheese Ball, 132
Parmesan Cream Spread, 165
Party Dip, 30
Richard's Garlic Dill Pickles, 142
Smoked Turkey Ball, 129
Stuffed Sweet Cherry Peppers, 28

Inspirations
A good dinner . . ., 76
A Recipe for Life, 156
Best Portion of Life, 104
Book of Life, 175
Business of Life, 96
Comes the Dawn, 71
Cooking with Love, 80
Desire Accomplished, 34
Enthusiasm, 130
Food and Friends, 35
Food Reflects the Soul, 207
Formula for Success, 70
Good Cooks, 181
Love What's Lovable, 196
Sharing, 105
Soothe the Savage, 68
Soul without Watchfulness, 85
Taste is . . ., 8
Thinking is . . ., 174
Truly Elegant Taste, 146
Turnpike to hearts, 94
We are shaped and fashioned, 206
Words of Wisdom, 21

Lamb
Bean and Sausage Stew, 159

Munchies
  Breadstick Snacks, 69
  Louisiana Cheese Crisps, 100
  Texas Trash, 152
Onions
  Crisp Sliced, 18
Pasta
  Baked Parmesan Cheese Noodles, 102
Pet Food
  Happy Birthday Puppa, 98
Pickles
  Melba's Garlic Sweet Pickles, 141
  Richard's Garlic Dill Pickles, 142
Pies
  Banana Cream Pie, 33
  Chocolate Icebox Pie, 123
  Coconut Cream Pie, 34
  Cream Cheese Pie, 147
  French Silk Pie, 101
  Fudge Pie, 50
  German Chocolate Pie, 128
  Graham Cracker Crust, 113
  Hershey Bar Pie, 112
  Key Lime Pie, 127
  Pecan Pie ... etc., 48
  Pie Crust, The Very Best You've Ever Made, 32
  Pie Crusts, 112
  Pumpkin Pie, 87
  Strawberry Icebox Pie, 123
  Strawberry Pie, 116
Pizza
  Pizza Pie, 171
Pork
  Baked Ham Hash, 157
  Barbequed Spam, 31
  Bean and Sausage Stew, 159
  Chicken Fried Steak, 63
  Escalloped Pork Chops, 75
  Ham & Cheese Rollups, 140
  Ham in Soups, 12
  Italian Sausage Sauce, 78
  Marinated Pork Chops, 205
  Mother's Hors d' oeuvres, 29
  Pigs -n- Blanket, 41
  Pork Roast, 9
  Rack of Spam, 30
  South Texas Pork Stew, 76
  Southern Baked Pork Cutlets, 196
  Stuffed Sweet Cherry Peppers, 28
  The Original Breakfast Tacos, 42
Potatoes
  Baked Potatoes ... Plus, 58
  Easy Potatoes Au Gratin, 198
  Green Potato Soup, 169
  Kentucky Style Potato Salad, 199
  Mashed, with Pork Gravy, 8
  New Potato Salad, 172
  Sweet Potato Pie, 86
  Sweet Potato Casserole, 131
Pudding
  Bread Pudding, 62
  Mother's Bread Puddin', 205
  Popcorn Puddin', 68
  Raisin Corn Pudding, 22
Quiche
  Crustless Quiche, 153
  My Mama's Hot Quiche, 110
Raisins
  About Raisins, 20
  Plumped Raisins, 20
  Raisin Corn Pudding, 22
Relish
  Corn Relish, 143
  Cranberry Relish, 91
  Pico de Gallo, 164
  Pico de Terry, 182
  Sweet Corn Relish, 94
Rice
  Broccoli Rice Casserole, 151
  Cheese Rice Casserole, 136
  Chili Rice, 150
  Dessert Rice, 188
Salad Dressings
  Fresh Basil, Vinegar & Oil Dressing, 92
  Home Made Garlic Croutons, 17
  Neiman Marcus Poppy Seed Dressing, 197

Orange Vinaigrette, 57
Pasta Dressing, 135
Richard's Special Dressing, 90
Russian Dressing, 111
Yogurt Dressing, 167

Salads
24 - Hour Icebox Salad, 90
Asparagus Salad, 129
Authentic Caesar Salad, 176
Carrot Jell-o Salad, 46
Corn Relish, 143
Cranberry Relish, 91
Curry Chicken with Melon, 167
Fresh Zuchini Salad, 110
Kentucky Style Potato Salad, 199
Lillian's Salad, 200
New Potato Salad, 172
My Orange Vinaigrette Salad, 57
Pico de Gallo, 164
Pico de Terry, 182
Reception Salad, 121
Richard's Pasta Salad, 135
Summer Avocado Salad, 96
Summer Stuffed Tomatoes, 104
Sweet Corn Relish, 94
Tomato Aspic, 19
Traditional Tuna Salad, 199
Tuna Salad — The World's Best, 21
Waldorf Salad, 40

Salmon
Easy Salmon Patties, 78
Salmon Croquettes, 194

Sandwiches
Jarlsberg Tuna Melt, 184

Sauces
Easy Salsa, 42
Garlic Sauce, 42
Italian Sauage Sauce, 78
Jarlsberg Cheese Fondue, 53
New Orleans Style Shrimp Sauce, 179
Pico de Terry, 182
Pig Sauce, 41
Plantation Sauce, 109
Remoulade Sauce, 155
Richard's Cheese Sauce, 45
Spicy Caper Mayonnaise, 79
Steak Sauce, 174
White Sauce, 204

Sauerkraut
Spiced Sauerkraut with Canadian Bacon, 88

Seasonings
About, 7
Adding Flavor, 14
Italian Herbs, 166
Oregano (cautions), 16
Salt vs. Vege-Sal, 14
Tips on Flavored Steam Veggies, 89

Shrimp
Louisiana Boiled Shrimp, 179
Marinated Shrimp, 97
Padre Island Shrimp Roast, 96

Side Dishes
Broccoli Rice Casserole, 151
Cheese Rice Casserole, 136
Chilli Rice, 150
Missippi Cheese Grits, 111

Soups
Bean Soup, 12
Black Bean Soup, 166
Canned, 12
Cheese Soup, 154
Cream Soups, 12
Easy Broccoli Cheese Soup, 203
Green Potato Soup, 169
Old Fashion Mushroom Soup, 201
Peanut Soup, 12
Soups On, 12
Starters, 12
Starting with Beef Bone, 15
Using Leftovers, 11

Spinach
Spinach in Mushroom Sauce, 109
Spinach in Sour Cream, 194

Spreads
Brandied Mixed Fruit Spread, 178

Squash
  Buttered Yellow Squash, 185
  Nuked Zucchini, 80
Tamales
  Tamale Pie, 163
  Texas Tamales, 161
Tea
  Neiman Marcus Spiced Tea, 180
This and That
  Brandied Mixed Fruit Spread, 178
  Richard's Unconventional Breakfast, 187
Tomatoes
  Fried Green Tomatoes, 160
  Summer Stuffed Tomatoes, 104
  Tomato Aspic, 19
Toppings
  Half & Half Topping, 146
  Sour Cream Topping, 147
  Whipped Cream, 87
Tuna
  Easy Tuna Casserole, 67
  Jarlsberg Tuna Melt, 184
  The World's Best Tuna Salad, 21
  Traditional Tuna Salad, 199
Turnip Greens
  Turnip Greens with Cornmeal Dumplings, 132
Vegetables
  A Different Green Bean Casserole, 206
  Alabama Corn Casserole, 177
  The Absolute Best Bar-B-Q Beans, 43 — 44
  Buttered Yellow Squash, 185
  Tender Cooked Cauliflower, 45—47
  Carrot Jell-o Salad, 46
  Catalina Carrot Coins, 45
  Cole-n-Sak, 74
  Cooked Cabbage, 44
  Corn & Onion, 22
  Delicious Artichokes, 93
  Easy Potatoes Au Gratin, 198
  Easy Salsa, 42
  Fried Green Tomatoes, 160
  Great Northern Beans, 87
  Green Bean Bundles, 95
  Green Bean Casserole, 116
  Green Bean Casserole II, 117
  Green Bean Casserole III, 117
  Mississippi Stir Fry w/Greens, 51
  Nuked Zucchini, 80
  Baked Potatoes ... Plus, 58
  Spanish Green Beans, 146
  Spiced Sauerkraut with Canadian Bacon, 88
  Spinach in Mushroom Sauce, 109
  Spinach in Sour Cream, 194
  Stuffed Sweet Cherry Peppers, 28
  Sweet Potato Casserole, 131
  Sweet Potato Pie, 86
  Tennessee Corn Casserole, 130
  Turnip Greens with Cornmeal Dumplings, 132

Soul Food Notes